PRAISE FOR *DID AMERICA HAVE a CHRISTIAN FOUNDING?*

"Mark's excellent book is so needed. Many do not understand the basics of religious freedom. Mark's book, though written by an academic, is a great beginning, helping citizens begin to understand the crucial issues of our first freedom."

—KELLY SHACKELFORD, ESQ., PRESIDENT, CEO, AND CHIEF COUNSEL, FIRST LIBERTY INSTITUTE

"In *Did America Have a Christian Founding?*, Mark David Hall debunks widespread secularist myths and provides a lively, illuminating account of the role of Christianity in our nation's founding. Everyone who cares about our nation's founding can benefit from this valuable and insightful book."

—LUKE GOODRICH, VICE PRESIDENT, THE BECKET FUND FOR RELIGIOUS LIBERTY, AND AUTHOR OF *FREE TO BELIEVE: THE BATTLE OVER RELIGIOUS LIBERTY IN AMERICA*

"Since Justice Hugo Black's opinion in *Everson v. Board of Education* (1947), we have been told that a deist 'wall of separation between church and state' defined the relationship between government and religion established by the American Founders with the Constitution, including the Bill of Rights. Now Mark David Hall, leading expert on American church-state relations and author of the best biography of Founder Roger Sherman, shows that Black erred, and wildly. The American Revolution was a Christian revolution, the American Founding was a Christian founding, and the religious freedom of the First Amendment is a product of Christian thought at the time of the Revolution. Freedom of religion was intended for people of all faiths, but it was not anti-religious. Hall gives us a bracing corrective to a pernicious myth—and shows us how his conclusions are applicable today."

—KEVIN R. C. GUTZMAN, JD, PHD, AUTHOR OF *THOMAS JEFFERSON: REVOLUTIONARY* AND *JAMES MADISON AND THE MAKING OF AMERICA*

"The American republic was not founded in 1787 as a unitary, confessional, Christian state. But it *was* founded within the context of an overwhelmingly Christian population, and nearly all the Founders adhered to, or were influenced by, Christian moral teachings and practices. Most importantly, the Founders recognized that if their new regime of ordered liberty was to survive and prosper, it must be sustained by the indispensable pillars of religion and morality. Professor Hall's lucid volume illuminates these often-overlooked influences on the Founders and corrects many modern misconceptions about their political philosophy and achievements."

—GEORGE H. NASH, HISTORIAN, LECTURER, AND AUTHOR OF *THE CONSERVATIVE INTELLECTUAL MOVEMENT IN AMERICA SINCE 1945*

"Mark David Hall has provided a decisive, readable, and scholarly answer to the perennially debated question, Did America have a Christian founding? Herein, a distinguished American historian demonstrates far beyond a reasonable doubt that America's Founders were deeply influenced by the Christian faith. If you have time to read only one book on the subject, this is categorically the one you should choose."

—PETER A. LILLBACK, PRESIDENT OF THE WESTMINSTER THEOLOGICAL SEMINARY, PHILADELPHIA, AND THE PROVIDENCE FORUM

"After years of reading overstatements from both sides of the Founding debate, I enjoyed Mark David Hall's calm and thorough analysis. Mind readers and diary extrapolaters may still fight over questions of sincerity and personal faithfulness, but Hall clearly shows what's most important: that Christian ideas profoundly influenced the Founders, and through them all of us."

—DR. MARVIN OLASKY, EDITOR IN CHIEF OF *WORLD* AND AUTHOR OF *FIGHTING FOR LIBERTY AND VIRTUE*

"In this beautiful book, Mark David Hall fully debunks the pervasive myth that America's founders were deists. As I turned each page, my smile grew larger to know that here, in a single short book, history was being set aright, in a way that should hush the voices of those who have too long declared that our founders were not really men of faith. As Dr. Hall ably demonstrates, America's founders were driven by a deep sense of religious conscience, founded in their Christian faith, to establish a new nation conceived in liberty."

—RODNEY K. SMITH, STIRLING CHAIR AND DIRECTOR OF THE CENTER FOR CONSTITUTIONAL STUDIES, UTAH VALLEY UNIVERSITY, AND AUTHOR OF *JAMES MADISON: THE FATHER OF RELIGIOUS LIBERTY*

"Carefully researched and skillfully nuanced, Mark David Hall's *Did America Have a Christian Founding?* challenges the view that America's founding was more secular than religious. For those who want to understand the influence of the Bible on the American founding, Hall offers a readable and compelling case for the linkages of Christian faith and American liberty."

—ROY L. PETERSON, PRESIDENT AND CEO, AMERICAN BIBLE SOCIETY

"In his new book, *Did America Have a Christian Founding?*, Mark David Hall makes the compelling case that the majority of the Founding Fathers were not deists who openly rejected Orthodox Christian doctrines, and who advocated the strict separation of church and state. On the contrary. Hall persuasively argues that—with the exception of Benjamin Franklin, Ethan Allen, and Thomas Paine—the Founders were influenced by Christian ideas, and that even Jefferson and Madison (who have often been portrayed as doctrinaire deists) did not want a high wall separating church and state. He also discusses the Christian faith and views on church-state relations of some of the lesser-known Founders, such as Roger Sherman, James Wilson, and John Witherspoon. While Christianity was not the only significant influence on the thought of America's Founders, Christianity had a profound influence on the founding generation. The Christian faith of the Founders, beginning with George Washington, influenced and shaped their political beliefs and actions.

Hall's beautifully written and immensely thoughtful new book should be read by anyone interested in the role of religion in the founding of the American Republic. Rich in its insight and analysis, Hall's book brilliantly illuminates the interplay of American politics and religion during the founding era, and explains how and why the Founders' ideas are still relevant to our understanding of the role that religion should play in American public life today."

—DAVID G. DALIN, SENIOR RESEARCH FELLOW, BRANDEIS
UNIVERSITY, AND AUTHOR OF *JEWISH JUSTICES OF THE SUPREME
COURT, FROM BRANDEIS TO KAGAN: THEIR LIVES AND LEGACIES*

"In *Did America Have a Christian Founding?*, Mark Hall grants the modern reader a window into the predominant worldview of our Constitution's many framers and ratifiers, through dozens of original sources and hundreds of scholarly references. In contrast to the bias-driven mythologies he exposes, Hall leads his readers to reasoned conclusions about historical truth through objective scholarship in the vein of storytelling. He is humble enough to acknowledge legitimate separationist claims, while bold enough to demonstrate how the preponderance of historical evidence begs an affirmative answer to his title question. With many implications for today's challenges, *Did America Have a Christian Founding?* is history that is relevant for our time."

—ROBERT LITTLEJOHN, PhD, COAUTHOR OF *WISDOM AND
ELOQUENCE: A CHRISTIAN PARADIGM FOR CLASSICAL LEARNING*

"Of debates about the principles of the American Founding there is no end; which is no surprise, since the character of our country has its origins in that period when America won its independence and established its Constitution. What is surprising is how many scholars enter the discussion with presuppositions that limit their field of vision and color even what they do see. Thus, in one standard version of the American founding, the fathers of our country were all in the grip of notions of political life variously characterized as liberal, secular, Enlightenment, and even anti-Christian. Evidence to the contrary, then, is either ignored or creatively reinterpreted to fit the scholars' presuppositions.

Mark David Hall comes to the study of the American founding without such blinders on. The result is a fresh look at the very real extent to which Christian thought and belief played a vital role in the making of our country. A veteran student of the founding with numerous books to his credit, Hall has written his latest book for any interested reader—yet his endnotes will satisfy the most rigorous demands of his fellow scholars. Hall does not counter one myth with another— there is no exaggerated case here for a 'pious nation kneeling around the altar'—but instead shows that the American devotion to freedom, limited government, constitutionalism, and the rule of law owe as much or more to the Christian character of our founding generation as to any putatively 'secular' philosophical sources. For the founders, freedom and faith were compatible, not at odds but mutually supportive. So they can and should be for us."

—MATTHEW J. FRANCK, ASSOCIATE DIRECTOR, JAMES MADISON PROGRAM IN AMERICAN IDEALS AND INSTITUTIONS, PRINCETON UNIVERSITY

"In this book, Professor Hall powerfully and thoroughly rebuts—claim by claim— the consistently errant assertions by a never-ending stream of prominent and popular commentators who report that the American Founding was a wholly secular and enlightenment affair. His work builds from his impressive thirty-year scholarly corpus on how the American Founding was importantly influenced by Protestant Christian theology and institutions. Here he convincingly shows that the putative hostility of the American Founders to Christianity and their embrace of a secular philosophy is 'unequivocally false' for all but a small handful of men and, in most cases, for only part of their lives, often years before or after the Founding period. Hall demonstrates that these claims about a secular founding are consistently made without convincing (or, in some cases, any) supporting evidence, in a manner that prevents the formation of an accurate understanding of America, then and now, to the detriment of all."

—BARRY ALAN SHAIN, PROFESSOR OF POLITICAL SCIENCE, COLGATE UNIVERSITY, AND AUTHOR OF THE MYTH OF AMERICAN INDIVIDUALISM: THE PROTESTANT ORIGINS OF AMERICAN POLITICAL THOUGHT

"Professor Hall examines the passionately debated question of whether America had a Christian founding, through the lens of honest scholarship for which he is known and respected. The result is a highly readable book for anyone who seeks a thoughtful and fair-minded evaluation of the Founders' understanding of Christianity, and its relationship to the national government that they established through the Constitution and made subject to the First Amendment."

—KIM COLBY, DIRECTOR, CENTER FOR LAW AND
RELIGIOUS FREEDOM, CHRISTIAN LEGAL SOCIETY

"This is a book we have badly needed for a long time, and Mark David Hall has performed a great public service in writing it. For too long the subject of Christianity's relationship to the American Founding has been needlessly obscured in a fog of misunderstanding, oversimplification, half-truth, and deliberate misrepresentation. Hall has cut through the fog, producing a work that not only builds on the most careful recent scholarship, but presents its findings in a remarkably accessible and persuasive way. For its clear and penetrating insights into the American past and present alike, this is a book that every thoughtful American needs to read."

—WILFRED M. MCCLAY, G. T. AND LIBBY BLANKENSHIP CHAIR
IN THE HISTORY OF LIBERTY, UNIVERSITY OF OKLAHOMA

"In this engaging book, Mark David Hall revisits the persistent myth that the American founding was a strictly secular, enlightenment project. Among the questions he investigates are: Were the American founders all deists who framed a godless Constitution? Did the founders erect a high wall of separation between church and state, restricting religion's role in public life? These are not questions merely of academic interest; rather, as Hall shows, they have immediate implications for law and public policy. His insightful, amply documented conclusions will inform the lay historian and seasoned scholar alike."

—DANIEL L. DREISBACH, PROFESSOR OF LEGAL STUDIES,
AMERICAN UNIVERSITY, AND AUTHOR OF *THOMAS JEFFERSON
AND THE WALL OF SEPARATION BETWEEN CHURCH AND STATE
AND READING THE BIBLE WITH THE FOUNDING FATHERS*

"A critically important work, Mark Hall's latest book demonstrates that a large number of America's Founders held deep Christian faith, and applied their beliefs to the Nation's foundational documents, speeches, and Constitutional provisions. Relying on original sources and texts, and written for the academic and the nonacademic alike, this book is for anyone who is interested in answering for themselves, Did America have a Christian founding?"

—Charlie Copeland, president, Intercollegiate Studies Institute

"As Mark Hall reminds us, the Bible did not provide a manual for the Constitution as a structure of governance. But the Jewish–Christian tradition provided the deep moral premises that underlay the Constitution, for it provided an account of the 'human person' and the rightful and wrongful ways for human beings to be governed. As Lincoln would say, 'nothing stamped with the Divine image and likeness was sent into the world to be trodden on, and degraded, and imbruted by its fellows.' What Christianity confirmed was that human beings were 'rights-bearing beings.' And that sense of things would underlie the claim to all of our natural and Constitutional rights, from the grand to the prosaic. It would encompass our right not to have our lives taken, our freedom restricted, or our earnings and property taken in a lawless way, without justification.

Mark Hall offers a bracing corrective to those scholars and writers who have somehow failed to notice the Jewish–Christian moral premises that thread through the Constitution. And he brings the insight that will also come as news to them: that our tradition of religious pluralism did not spring from a 'secular' understanding that began simply by denying that any particular religion has a plausible claim to truth. That pluralism, and religious tolerance, sprang rather from our religious tradition. It was anchored in the understanding that creatures of reason should come to an understanding of God through their reflection and reason, not through coercion. And that is not a moral understanding that comes along with just anything that calls itself 'religion.' The American understanding of religious freedom made room for people making their way to God in their own way, but as Hall points out, 'religious' freedom made no sense if a new view of religion managed to dispense with God. Not just any local god, but the one recognized at the very beginning in the Declaration of Independence: the Author of the laws of nature, including the moral laws, and the Creator who endowed us with rights. The irony is that a regime that began with that understanding of God was more likely to protect the freedom of Buddhists and Unitarians, and in its large nature, even atheists."

—Hadley Arkes, Edward Ney Professor of Jurisprudence Emeritus, Amherst College, and director, James Wilson Institute

DID
AMERICA
HAVE A
CHRISTIAN
FOUNDING?

DID AMERICA HAVE A CHRISTIAN FOUNDING?

SEPARATING MODERN MYTH FROM HISTORICAL TRUTH

MARK DAVID HALL

NELSON
BOOKS

An Imprint of Thomas Nelson

Published in Nashville, Tennessee, by Nelson Books, an imprint of Thomas Nelson. Nelson Books and Thomas Nelson are registered trademarks of HarperCollins Christian Publishing, Inc.

Thomas Nelson titles may be purchased in bulk for educational, business, fund-raising, or sales promotional use. For information, please e-mail SpecialMarkets@ThomasNelson.com.

Scripture quotations are taken from the King James Version. Public domain.

ISBN 978-1-4002-1111-1 (eBook)

Library of Congress Control Number: 2018967245

ISBN 978-1-4002-1110-4 (HC)

Printed in the United States of America

19 20 21 22 23 LSC 10 9 8 7 6 5 4 3 2 1

To Miriam

CONTENTS

Introduction: The Problem | xv

CHAPTER 1
The Myth of the Founders' Deism | 1

CHAPTER 2
The United States Does Not Have a Godless Constitution | 21

CHAPTER 3
Thomas Jefferson, James Madison, and the First Amendment | 57

CHAPTER 4
The Founders Believed Civic Authorities Should Protect,
Promote, and Encourage Religion and Morality | 87

CHAPTER 5
Christianity, Religious Liberty, and Religious Exemptions | 121

Conclusion | 149
Acknowledgments | 155
Notes | 161
About the Author | 211

THE PROBLEM

S cholars and popular authors routinely assert that America's founders were deists who desired the strict separation of church and state. University of Chicago law professor Geoffrey Stone, for example, wrote that "deistic beliefs played a central role in the framing of the American republic" and that the "Founding generation viewed religion, and particularly religion's relation to government, through an Enlightenment lens that was deeply skeptical of orthodox Christianity."[1] Similarly, historian Frank Lambert contends that the "significance of the Enlightenment and Deism for the birth of the American republic, and especially the relationship between church and state within it, can hardly be overstated."[2] Even prominent Christian college professors such as Richard T. Hughes argue that "most of the American founders embraced some form of Deism, not historically orthodox Christianity."[3] Examples of authors who make such statements may be multiplied almost indefinitely.[4]

These claims are patently and unequivocally false. This book demonstrates why, revealing the hollowness of assertions that most of America's founders were deists; that they created a "godless" Constitution; that Thomas Jefferson and James Madison desired to build a high wall of separation between church and state; that the founders thought governments should never encourage religion; and that they advocated religious liberty because they were children of the Enlightenment. In addition to showing why and how these claims are wrong, I argue that America's founders were influenced in significant ways by Christian ideas when they declared independence from Great Britain, drafted constitutions, and passed laws to protect religious liberty.

Scholars and popular authors have spent a great deal of ink debating different variations of the question that gives this book its title: Did America have a Christian founding?[5] This book reveals that the answer is a resounding yes. Moreover, it shows that this is good news for all Americans—even for those who adhere to non-Christian religions or to no faith at all.

WHY IT MATTERS

A little more than a hundred years ago, Henry Ford famously proclaimed that "history is bunk."[6] America's founders disagreed. The influential but often overlooked signer of the Declaration, drafter of the Constitution, and early Supreme Court Justice James Wilson observed in his law lectures at the College of Philadelphia (now the University of Pennsylvania) that "of all governments, those are the best, which, by the natural effect of their constitutions, are frequently renewed or drawn back to their first principles."[7] The founders believed that reflecting on the basic ideas from which the authors of a constitutional order drew was crucial to determining how best to proceed in the present. This does not mean that contemporary problems can be solved simply by asking, What would the founders do? But it does suggest that we do well to consider the principles that animated the men and women who helped win American independence and created our constitutional republic.[8]

Supreme Court justices have made it clear that history matters when interpreting the Constitution. Most judicial conservatives, of course, insist that the Constitution must be interpreted according to the original intent or original understanding of the founders.[9] But this view is not taken solely by conservatives. When it comes to the First Amendment's Religion Clauses—"Congress shall make no law respecting an establishment of religion, or prohibiting the free exercise thereof"—progressives and conservatives alike agree, in the words of the liberal Justice Wiley Rutledge, that "no provision of the Constitution is more closely tied to or given content by its generating history than the Religious Clause of the First Amendment. It is at once the refined product and the terse summation of that history."[10] That agreement notwithstanding, liberal justices often distort the founders' views, as we shall see. But with few exceptions, all justices agree that history must inform our understanding of what the Constitution requires with respect to religious liberty and church-state relations.[11]

More broadly, America's founders and their perspectives continue to matter in our nation's political discourse. Civic leaders of all stripes appeal to the founders' views to support contemporary policies. For instance, President George W. Bush argued that racial discrimination violates America's founding principles.[12] Politicians are even more likely to refer to the founders' views when discussing religious liberty, as illustrated by every recent president's Religious Freedom Day proclamation.[13] In 2015, President Obama observed,

The First Amendment prohibits the Government from establishing religion. It protects the right of every person to practice their faith how they choose, to change their faith, or to practice no faith at all, and to do so free from persecution and fear. This religious freedom allows faith to flourish, and our Union is stronger because a vast array of religious communities coexist peacefully with mutual respect for one another. Since the age of Jefferson and Madison, brave women and men of faith have challenged our conscience; today, our Nation continues to be shaped by people of every religion and of no religion, bringing us closer to our founding ideals. As heirs to this proud legacy of liberty, we must remain vigilant in our efforts to safeguard these freedoms.[14]

Like liberal Supreme Court justices, President Obama did not always adhere to the founders' vision for religious liberty. For instance, his administration showed little concern for this important right when it required businesses to provide contraceptives and abortifacients to employees even when the business owners had religious objections to doing so.[15] It also offered a rare challenge to the doctrine of ministerial exception, a legal protection that holds that religious groups should be free to choose, in the words of Chief Justice John Roberts, "who will preach their beliefs, teach their faith, and carry out their mission."[16] But the principle remains: Democrats and Republicans, judicial conservatives and liberals, agree that the founders' views on religious liberty and church-state relations matter for contemporary law and public policy. The problem is not the principle that we should look to the founders for guidance, but the profoundly distorted picture of their views promoted by many scholars, popular authors, and judges. This book sets the record straight.

WHAT WOULD A CHRISTIAN
FOUNDING LOOK LIKE?

Before progressing, let's define a few terms. It might help to begin by asking what, exactly, would constitute a *Christian* founding?

One possibility is simply that the founders *identified* themselves as Christians, which they clearly did. In 1776, every colonist, with the exception of about two thousand Jews, identified himself or herself as a Christian.[17] Approximately 98 percent of them were Protestants, and the remaining 2 percent were Roman Catholics.[18] But these facts alone are not particularly useful. These men and women may have been bad Christians, may have been Christians significantly influenced by non-Christian ideas, or may even have been Christians self-consciously attempting to create a secular political order. As we shall see, there are good reasons to reject these possibilities, but even so, it is necessary to dig deeper.

A second possibility is that the founders were all *sincere* Christians. This would be a more interesting finding, yet sincerity is difficult for scholars, or anyone else, to judge. In most cases, the historical record gives us little with which to work. Even if we can determine, say, that a particular founder was a member, a regular attender, and even an officer in a church, it does not necessarily mean that he was a sincere Christian. Perhaps he did these things simply because society expected it of him.

Third, we might mean that the founders were *orthodox* Christians. In some cases—for example, with Samuel Adams, Patrick Henry, John Jay, Roger Sherman, and John Witherspoon—there is abundant evidence that they embraced and articulated orthodox Christian ideas. But the lack of records makes it difficult to speak with confidence on this issue with respect to some founders. Nevertheless, because of the many misleading statements on the subject, I demonstrate that there is *no* evidence to support the popular claim that many or most of the founders rejected orthodox Christianity or were deists.[19]

A fourth possibility is that the founders *acted* like Christians in their private or public lives. Some historians have argued that the founding cannot be called Christian because some founders did not join churches, take communion, or remain faithful to their spouses.[20] Moreover, they say, in their public capacity the founders did not act in a Christian manner because they did things such as fight an unjust war against England and did not immediately abolish slavery.[21] In some cases, these critiques do not take into account historical context, such as the difficulty of joining Calvinist churches in eighteenth-century America, which complicates claims regarding low church membership. In other cases, these critiques neglect the traditional Christian teaching that even saints sin. If the standard of being a Christian is moral perfection, no one has ever been a Christian.

A final possibility for the meaning of a "Christian founding" is that the founders were *influenced* by Christian ideas. I believe this is the most reasonable way to approach the question, Did America have a *Christian* founding?[22] In doing so, it is important to note that nominal Christians might be influenced by Christian ideas, just as it is possible for an orthodox Christian to be influenced by non-Christian ideas. Book after book has been written about whether the founders were most influenced by Lockean liberalism, classical republicanism, the Scottish Enlightenment, and so on. I contend that an excellent case can be made that Christianity had a profound influence on the founding generation.[23]

What Constitutes America's *Founding?*

It is often assumed that America was founded in the late eighteenth century, but some authors have argued that our "nation begins not in 1776, but more than one hundred fifty years earlier."[24] Few doubt that New England Puritans, for example, were serious Christians attempting to create, in the words of Massachusetts governor John Winthrop, "a city upon a hill" (see Matt. 5:14).[25] Puritans separated church and state, but they thought the two institutions should work in tandem to support, protect, and promote true Christianity.[26] For instance, Massachusetts Bay's 1647 penal code stipulated that:

1. If any man after legal conviction shall have or worship any other God, but the LORD GOD: he shall be put to death. *Exod.* 22:20; *Deut.* 13:6 & 10; *Deut.* 17:2, 6.
2. If any man or woman be a WITCH, that is, hath or consults with a familiar spirit, they shall be put to death. *Exod.* 22:18; *Levit.* 20:27; *Deut.* 18:10–11.[27]

On a more positive note, parents and masters were required to teach children and apprentices to read so they could read the Bible themselves, and fathers were required to "catechize their children and servants in the grounds & principles of Religion."[28] By any measure, the Puritans made every effort to create a godly commonwealth.

Most scholars agree that colonies in New England (with the partial exception of Rhode Island) were founded on Christian principles. However, some deny that this was the case for other colonies. The historian John Fea, for instance, contends that "the real appeal of

Jamestown was economic opportunity and the very real possibility of striking it rich."[29] It is certainly true that colonists were attracted to the New World by economic opportunity (in New England as well as in the South), but still, even in the southern colonies, the protection and promotion of Christianity were more important than many authors assume. For instance, Virginia's 1610 legal code begins:

> Whereas his Majesty, like himself a most zealous prince, has in his own realms a principal care of true religion and reverence to God and has always strictly commanded his generals and governors, with all his forces wheresoever, to let their ways be, like his ends, for the glory of God . . .[30]

The first three articles of this document go on to state that the colonists have embarked on a "sacred cause," to mandate regular church attendance, and to proclaim that anyone who speaks impiously against the Trinity or who blasphemes God's name will be put to death.[31]

Even tolerant Quaker Pennsylvania accepted the idea that the government should protect and promote Christianity and Christian values. The *Charter of Liberties and Frame of Government of the Province of Pennsylvania* (1681) begins by making it clear that God has ordained government, and it even quotes Romans 13 to this effect. Article 38 of the document lists "offenses against God" that may be punished by the magistrate, including

> swearing, cursing, lying, profane talking, drunkenness, drinking of healths, obscene words, incest, sodomy . . . stage-plays, cards, dice, May-games, gamesters, masques, revels, bull-baiting, cock-fighting,

bear-baiting, and the like, which excite the people to rudeness, cruelty, looseness, and irreligion.[32]

A survey of early colonial constitutions and laws reveals many similar provisions. At least nine of the thirteen colonies had established churches, and virtually all the rest required officeholders to be Christians—or, in many cases, Protestants. Pennsylvania, for instance, expected officeholders to be "such as possess faith in Jesus Christ."[33]

If one is to understand American history, it is important to have a proper appreciation for the nation's Christian colonial roots. Few serious scholars deny that the early colonists were committed Christians, whose constitutions, laws, and practices reflected the influence of their faith (especially in New England). But the historical debate becomes far more heated with respect to Christianity's role in the War of Independence and the establishment of the constitutional order under which our nation still operates. For this reason, in this book, I focus almost exclusively on the late eighteenth century.

WHY THIS BOOK?

I have written or edited a dozen academic books, most of which consider in one way or another the relationship between Christianity and politics/law in America's founding. These books, along with works by like-minded students of America's founding, have encouraged jurists and academics to reconsider the role of religion in the era, but none of our works have been read widely outside our disciplines.

In this book, I distill thirty years of scholarly work on Christianity's role in the American founding into an accessible resource for nonacademics. I challenge a number of assertions that are found regularly in scholarly and popular books. Simply getting American history right is a worthy goal in its own right, but in this case, it also has immediate implications for law and public policy as political leaders and jurists continue to look to America's founders for guidance. This is especially true with respect to religious liberty and church-state relations.

In academic books, it is customary to spend a great deal of time engaging the work of other scholars, in part to demonstrate that one is aware of the most important secondary literature and also to show that one's interpretations are superior to those of other scholars. Other than quoting authors I am criticizing to make it clear that I am not attacking straw men, I spend little time engaging other works *about* the founding.[34] Instead, in each chapter, I make arguments based on laws, letters, debates, official state papers, and other primary source documents *from* the founding era. I carefully document quotations from these sources so that interested readers can check to make sure I am using them fairly. I occasionally cite good secondary sources in the endnotes and conclude each chapter by offering suggestions for further reading. These features permit those who would like to dig deeper to do so.

A book like this may appear at first glance to be an exercise in Christian triumphalism. I am a practicing Christian (although my pastor says I need more practice), and I am also a proud American. But I hope it is clear, by the end of the book, that I have provided a fair and balanced account of Christianity's role in America's founding. Anyone who desires to understand this critical era simply must grasp the pervasive influence of religion at the time. Similarly, it would be foolhardy to ignore Islam when considering the history and politics of Saudi Arabia.

Practically, and positively, a central argument of this book is that America's founders drew from their Christian convictions to create a constitutional order that benefits *all* Americans, not just Christians. Their convictions led them, for example, to carefully limit the national government's power, value checks and balances, support the rule of law, and protect a robust conception of religious liberty. There were few non-Christians in late eighteenth-century America,[35] but there were some, and most of America's founders were convinced that the right of these non-Christians to believe and act according to the dictates of their consciences must be protected.

Consider, for instance, George Washington's 1790 letter to the "Hebrew Congregation" in Newport, Rhode Island. He wrote to this tiny religious minority that:

All possess alike liberty of conscience and immunities of citizenship. It is now no more that toleration is spoken of, as if it was by the indulgence of one class of people, that another enjoyed the exercise of their inherent natural rights. For happily the Government of the United States, which gives to bigotry no sanction, to persecution no assistance requires only that they who live under its protection should demean themselves as good citizens, in giving it on all occasions their effectual support.

. . . May the Children of the Stock of Abraham, who dwell in this land, continue to merit and enjoy the good will of the other Inhabitants; while every one shall sit in safety under his own vine and fig tree, and there shall be none to make him afraid. May the father of all mercies scatter light and not darkness in our paths, and make us all in our several vocations useful here, and in his own due time and way everlastingly happy.[36]

This letter, from the era's one indispensable man, reflects well the founders' understanding that the religious convictions of all citizens must be respected. Yet it also illustrates the reality that America's founders did not think religion must be driven from the public square. In their book on Washington's faith, Peter Lillback and Jerry Newcombe identify nine scriptural references in this letter alone.[37] One of them is Micah 4:4, which reads "But they shall sit every man under his vine and under his fig tree; and none shall make them afraid: for the mouth of the LORD of hosts hath spoken it." This was one of George Washington's favorite verses; we have records of him quoting or paraphrasing it at least forty times.[38] Like other founders, Washington's faith influenced his political beliefs and actions, and all Americans—from Jewish citizens in the eighteenth century to Sikh citizens today—have benefited from this fact.

CHAPTER 1

THE MYTH OF THE FOUNDERS' DEISM[1]

The Founding Fathers were at most deists—they believed
God created the world, then left it alone to run.
GORDON WOOD, AMERICAN HERITAGE MAGAZINE

The founding fathers themselves, largely deists
in their orientation and sympathy.
EDWIN GAUSTAD, A DOCUMENTARY HISTORY OF RELIGION IN AMERICA

The Founding Fathers were . . . skeptical men of the Enlightenment
who questioned each and every received idea they had been taught.
BROOKE ALLEN, MORAL MINORITY

The God of the founding fathers was a benevolent deity, not far removed
from the God of eighteenth-century Deists or nineteenth-century
Unitarians. . . . They were not, in any traditional sense, Christian.
MARK A. NOLL, NATHAN O. HATCH, AND GEORGE M. MARSDEN,
THE SEARCH FOR CHRISTIAN AMERICA

America's Founders were philosophical radicals.
MATTHEW STEWART, NATURE'S GOD: THE HERETICAL
ORIGINS OF THE AMERICAN REPUBLIC[2]

Scholars and popular authors regularly assert that America's founders were deists. They support these claims by describing the religious views of the following men: Benjamin Franklin, George Washington, John Adams, Thomas Jefferson, James Madison, Thomas Paine, Alexander Hamilton, and Ethan Allen. On rare occasion, they reach beyond this select fraternity to include another founder, and they almost inevitably concede that not *all* founders were as enlightened as the ones they profile. However, they leave the distinct impression that most founders, and certainly the important ones, were deists.

In the eighteenth century, deism referred to an intellectual movement that emphasized the role of reason in discerning religious truth. Deists rejected traditional Christian doctrine such as the incarnation, virgin birth, atonement, resurrection, Trinity, divine inspiration of the Holy Scriptures, and miracles. For present purposes, this last point is critical; unlike most Christians, deists did not think God intervenes in the affairs of men and nations. In Alan Wolfe's words, they believed that "God set the world in motion and then abstained from human affairs."[3] In this chapter, I demonstrate that there is virtually no evidence that America's founders embraced such views.

CIVIC LEADERS WHO PUBLICLY EMBRACED DEISM

Given the numerous powerful and clear claims that the founders were deists, it is striking that there are few instances of civic leaders in the era openly embracing deism or rejecting orthodox Christian doctrines.[4] In 1725, during his first English sojourn, Benjamin Franklin published an essay entitled "A Dissertation on Liberty and Necessity, Pleasure and Pain," in which he concluded that "Vice and Virtue were empty Distinctions."[5] Deists emphasized the importance of morality, so the essay is not evidence of deism. But assuming Franklin was serious (often a dangerous assumption), the work is an example of a founder publicly rejecting a basic tenet of orthodox Christianity. Yet it is noteworthy that even as a young man, Franklin rapidly concluded that the essay "might have an ill Tendency," and he destroyed most copies of it before they could be distributed.[6]

In his autobiography, begun in 1771 and not published until after his death, Franklin acknowledged that he fell under the influence of deism as a young man. He noted his regret that his religious arguments "perverted" some of his friends. In his later years, Franklin may have moved toward more traditional religious views.[7] In the Constitutional Convention of 1787, he reflected that "the longer I live, the more convincing proofs I see of this truth—*that God governs the affairs of men*"[8] (emphasis original). Three years later, he wrote a letter to Yale president Ezra Stiles in which he affirmed many traditional Christian doctrines, but admitted he had "some doubts" about the divinity of Jesus of Nazareth.[9] As with many founders, Franklin's religious beliefs changed throughout his life. It seems reasonable, however, to classify him as a founder who both publicly and privately rejected or questioned some tenets of orthodox Christianity.

Ethan Allen, leader of the Green Mountain Boys, hero of Fort Ticonderoga, and advocate of statehood for Vermont, published the first American book advocating deism in 1784, *Reason: The Only Oracle of Man*. It sold fewer than two hundred copies, and after its publication, Allen played no role in American politics. Even modern authors sympathetic to Allen's views recognize that he was a "disorganized and stylistically clumsy writer," and that the book never achieved great influence.[10]

A decade later, Thomas Paine published his famous defense of deism, *The Age of Reason*. Paine was born and raised in England, and lived only twenty of his seventy-two years in America, so one can reasonably ask if he should be counted as an American founder. The book was written and first published in Europe. Although it sold reasonably well in the United States, America's civic leaders' reactions to it were almost uniformly negative.[11] Samuel Adams wrote his old ally a personal letter denouncing it, and John Adams, John Witherspoon, William Paterson, and John Jay each criticized the book.[12] Benjamin Rush called it "absurd and impious," Charles Carroll condemned Paine's "blasphemous writings against the Christian religion," and Connecticut jurist Zephaniah Swift wrote that we "cannot sufficiently reprobate the beliefs of Thomas Paine in his attack on Christianity."[13] Elias Boudinot and Patrick Henry went so far as to write book-length rebuttals of it.[14] When Paine returned to America, he was vilified because of the book. Indeed, with the exception of Jefferson and a few others, he was abandoned by all of his old friends. When he passed away in 1809, he had to be buried on a farm because even the tolerant Quakers refused to let him be interred in their church cemetery; only six mourners came to his funeral.[15]

Some founders may have secretly approved of *The Age of Reason* but criticized it for political reasons. Yet the overwhelmingly negative reaction to the work says a great deal about American religious and political culture in the late eighteenth century. Whatever attraction deism may have had for a select few, clearly the American public was not ready to embrace such teachings or political leaders who advocated heterodox ideas. With the exception of Franklin, Allen, and Paine, I am unaware of any civic leaders in the era who clearly and publicly rejected orthodox Christianity or embraced deism. There may be others, but those who claim the founders were deists give little or no evidence that they exist.

CIVIC LEADERS WHO PRIVATELY EMBRACED DEISM

Thomas Jefferson definitely rejected orthodox Christianity, but he went to great lengths to keep his religious views far from the public. Virtually all the texts that reveal his true beliefs were letters written to family members or close friends, and he often asked that they be kept private; in some cases, they were never sent, presumably because he was not sure the recipients could be trusted. An excellent example is an 1819 missive from Jefferson to William Short, where he rejected doctrines "invented by ultra-Christian sects" such as "the immaculate conception of Jesus, His deification, the creation of the world by Him, His miraculous powers, His resurrection and visible ascension, His corporeal presence in the Eucharist, the Trinity, original sin, atonement, regeneration, election, orders of Hierarchy, etc."[16]

Jefferson was a skeptic, but he realized that publicly advocating his religious views would be political suicide. Indeed, relatively minor lapses from his rule of secrecy, such as when he wrote in *Notes on the State of*

Virginia (1784) that "it does me no injury for my neighbor to say there are twenty gods, or no god. It neither picks my pocket nor breaks my leg," came close to costing him the election of 1800.[17]

John Adams was a lifelong Congregationalist who believed it appropriate for the state to support and encourage Christianity. He respected the Bible's moral teachings, as indicated by an 1816 letter where he wrote, "The Ten Commandments and the Sermon on the Mount contain my Religion."[10] Yet, in an 1813 letter to his son, he made it clear that he rejected the divinity of Christ: "An incarnate God!!! An eternal, self-existent, omnipresent omniscient Author of this stupendous Universe suffering on a Cross!!! My Soul starts with horror, at the Idea."[19] Like Jefferson, Adams kept his religious views extremely private. Indeed, the public's perception that he was a Calvinist who would impose a national church on the American people contributed to his losing the election of 1800.[20] But he nevertheless must be numbered among those founders who privately rejected Christian orthodoxy.

THE OTHER USUAL SUSPECTS

Three other founders are regularly referred to as deists: Washington, Madison, and Hamilton. Yet, to my knowledge, no writer has ever produced a public or private journal entry, letter, or essay showing that these men rejected Christianity or embraced deism. The argument that they did so is based almost entirely on negative evidence, resting on some combination of observations that they seldom used familiar biblical appellations for God or Jesus Christ, did not regularly attend church, chose not to become communicants, and/or did not always act in a moral manner.

In the case of George Washington, for instance, authors such as David Holmes argue that Washington referred to God with "Deistic terms [such] as 'Providence,' 'Heaven,' 'the Deity,' 'the Supreme Being,' 'the Grand Architect,' 'the Author of all Good,' and 'the Great Ruler of Events.'"[21] Yet, as I show below, indisputably orthodox Christians regularly used such appellations. On the surface, Washington's refusal to take communion suggests that he was not a serious Christian; however, as John Fea points out, this "was not uncommon among eighteenth-century Anglicans," and Washington may have done so because he "did not believe he was worthy to participate in the sacrament."[22]

Writing about Washington's religious beliefs is a virtual cottage industry, so I cannot assess and engage every argument about his faith here. Yet it is worth reemphasizing that none of the authors who claim Washington was a deist has cited a text where he rejected a basic tenet of orthodox Christianity. I have scoured Washington's works and have found one possibility, but I believe it should be treated with care. On March 31, 1791, Jefferson drafted and Washington signed a condolence letter to the emperor of Morocco that includes the sentence: "May that God, whom we both adore, bless your Imperial Majesty with long life, Health and Success, and have you always, great and magnanimous Friend, under his holy keeping."[23] Conflating the God of Christianity and the God of Islam is problematic from a traditional Christian perspective, yet given the diplomatic context, it seems imprudent to read too much into this missive.

Washington is sometimes accused of having an extramarital affair, and there is no doubt that Alexander Hamilton did so.[24] Some writers cite such actions as evidence that particular founders were not serious or orthodox Christians. But this line of argument neglects the traditional Christian teaching that even godly men and women continue to struggle with sin and fall short of moral perfection.

Madison was intensely private about his religious beliefs, so those who assert he was a deist often cite secondhand accounts to support their claims. For instance, the Anglican bishop William Meade recollected twenty years after Madison's death, "I was never at Mr. Madison's but once, and then our conversation took such a turn though not designed on my part as to call forth some expressions and arguments which left the impression on my mind that his creed was not strictly regulated by the Bible."[25] Such evidence should not be dismissed, but it needs to be treated with caution. In this case, one should not read too much into an "impression" made by someone who visited Madison's home only once. And it is not self-evident what Meade meant by Madison's creed not being "strictly regulated by the Bible."

It should come as little surprise that authors who rely on accounts such as Bishop Meade's often ignore or dismiss secondhand accounts that the founders were pious, orthodox Christians. For instance, John Marshall, the great chief justice, wrote that the general was a "sincere believer in the Christian faith, and a truly devout man."[26] Similarly, a Frenchman who knew Washington said, "Every day of the year, he rises at five in the morning; as soon as he is up, he dresses, then prays reverently to God."[27] Other similar accounts by people who knew him attest to Washington's piety, but they are regularly ignored by those who would label him a "cool deist" or a "lukewarm Episcopalian."[28]

Virtually every author who argues that the founders were deists cites Washington, Madison, and Hamilton as examples. Each of these men wrote a great deal, and scholars have recovered many of their papers. Washington's collected papers are projected to fill ninety volumes, Madison's fifty, and Hamilton's twenty-seven.[29] Yet contemporary writers have not cited a single instance where these founders clearly rejected a basic tenet of orthodox Christianity or embraced deism. I agree that some of their actions or inactions suggest, at least at certain points in their lives, that they were not pious, godly men. I also think it highly unlikely that if Washington were alive today he "would freely associate with the Bible-believing branch of evangelical Christianity that is having such a positive influence upon our nation," as Tim LaHaye asserted.[30] To question whether these founders were deists is not to claim that they were pious, evangelical Christians. Yet it is a different thing altogether to make the affirmative claim that they were deists. In the absence of more compelling evidence, students of the founding should avoid, or at least carefully qualify, such assertions.

But Surely There Must Be Others

For reasons of space I have focused on civic leaders usually discussed by those who claim that the founders were deists. Other founders occasionally put forward as deists include Benjamin Rush, Gouverneur Morris, Timothy Pickering, Joel Barlow, James Monroe, George Wythe, Thomas Young, and, prior to his 1808 conversion, Noah Webster.[31] I will not discuss these men here, but I will note, first, that in most cases there is little attempt to present evidence that they were deists; and, second, my own investigations reveal that in many instances the case is quite weak (usually relying on negative evidence). Because literally hundreds of men played important roles in the War of Independence and the creation of America's constitutional order, other deists will likely be discovered. But given the numerous, regular, and unqualified claims that "most" founders were deists, it is remarkable how little *evidence* there is that more than a handful of founders merit this distinction.

WAIT A MINUTE . . .

So far I have considered evidence, or the lack thereof, that the founders embraced deism or rejected basic tenets of orthodox Christianity. Before proceeding, I should note that if deism includes the idea that "God set the world in motion and then abstained from human affairs," it is possible that only one of these men, Ethan Allen, was a deist. With the exception of Allen, all the founders regularly called deists are clearly on record speaking or writing about God's intervention in the affairs of men and nations.[32]

George Washington, for instance, referred to "Providence" at least 270 times in his writings.[33] A good example is a 1755 letter to his brother, penned during the French and Indian War:

> I have heard since my arrival at this place, a circumstantial account of my death and dying speech. I take this early opportunity of contradicting the first, and of assuring you that I have not, as yet, composed the latter. But by the all-powerful dispensation of Providence, I have been protected beyond all human probability; I had 4 bullets through my coat, and two horses shot under me yet escaped unhurt although death was leveling my companions on every side of me.[34]

His successor, John Adams, routinely invoked Providence as well, such as when he wrote to his wife that "I must submit all my hopes and fears, to an overruling Providence, in which, unfashionable as the Faith may be, I firmly believe."[35] Jefferson did not refer to God's intervention in human affairs as often as his two predecessors, but he did so on occasion. His first inaugural address, for instance, included the line: "may that Infinite Power which rules the destinies of the universe lead our councils to what is best, and give them a favorable issue for your peace and prosperity."[36]

Early in his life, Franklin was perhaps more skeptical than any other founder, but by the end of his life, he seemed to believe in Providence. In the Constitutional Convention, he noted that, "in the beginning of the contest with Great Britain, when we were sensible of danger, we had daily prayer in this room for the divine protection.—Our prayers, Sir, were heard, and they were graciously answered . . . the longer I live, the more convincing proofs I see of this truth—*that God governs the affairs of men*"[37] (emphasis original). Franklin was the oldest delegate at the Convention, and his proposal to open each day in prayer was seconded by Roger Sherman, an indisputably pious man who was the second oldest member.[38] The delegates did not act on the suggestion, but Madison nevertheless discerned God's involvement in the proceedings.[39] In *Federalist* No. 37, he wrote: "It is impossible, for the man of pious reflection, not to perceive in it [the Constitutional Convention] a finger of that Almighty Hand, which has been so frequently and signally extended to our relief in the critical stages of the revolution."[40] (Despite this and another reference to the Deity in *Federalist* No. 37, and three mentions of "Providence" in *Federalist* No. 2, Isaac Kramnick and R. Laurence Moore still assert that *The Federalist Papers* "fail to mention God anywhere."[41])

Hamilton's religious views shifted throughout his life, but at least in his early and later years, he gave evidence of believing that God intervenes in the affairs of men and nations. For instance, shortly before his death, he wrote to an unknown recipient, encouraging him or her to "Arraign not the dispensations of Providence—they must be Founded in wisdom and goodness; and when they do not suit us, it must be because there is some fault in ourselves which deserves chastisement, or because there is a kind intent to correct in us some vice or failing of which, perhaps, we may not be conscious, or because the general plan requires that we should suffer partial ill."[42]

Even the infidel Thomas Paine wrote in *The American Crisis*:

The vast extension of America makes her of too much value in the scale of Providence, to be cast, like a pearl before swine, at the feet of an European island; and of much less consequence would it be that Britain were sunk in the sea than that America should miscarry. There has been such a chain of extraordinary events in the discovery of this country at first, in the peopling and planting it afterwards, in the rearing and nursing it to its present state, and in the protection of it through the present war, that no man can doubt, but Providence hath some nobler end to accomplish than the gratification of the petty Elector of Hanover, or the ignorant and insignificant King of Britain.[43]

Of course, some founders wrote or spoke of God intervening in human history more than others, and it is always possible that some did so simply for rhetorical effect. This is almost certainly the case with Paine. Yet, it is noteworthy that most authors who claim the founders were deists ignore these and other clear statements by them that God intervenes in the affairs of men and nations. If deism includes the idea that "God set the world in motion and then abstained from human affairs," then the number of civic leaders in the American founding who were deists may be only one, Ethan Allen; and other than his significant military victory at Fort Ticonderoga, his role in the American founding was minimal.

GOD WORDS?

One of America's most significant founding documents, the Declaration of Independence, affirms the founders' "reliance on the protection of divine Providence." The text refers to God three other times, most critically in the stirring proposition that "We hold these truths to be self-evident: that all men are created equal; that they are endowed by their Creator, with certain unalienable rights; that among these are life, liberty and the pursuit of happiness." The Declaration mentions as well "the laws of nature of nature's God" and closes by "appealing to the Supreme Judge of the world."[44]

Some scholars have argued that the use of "distant" or "vague and generic God-language," such as "Nature's God," "Creator," and "Providence," is evidence that the founders were deists.[45] It may be the case that deists regularly referred to God in this fashion, but, as I've noted, so did indisputably orthodox Christians. For instance, the Westminster Standards, a classic Reformed (Calvinist) confession of faith, refer to the Deity as "the Supreme Judge," "the great Creator of all things," "the first cause," "righteous judge," "God the Creator," and "the supreme Lord and King of all the world," both in the original 1647 version and the 1788 American revision. The Westminster Standards also regularly refer to "God's Providence," and even proclaim that "the light of nature showeth that there is a God."[46] Similarly, Isaac Watts, the "father of English Hymnody," called the Deity "nature's God" in a poem about Psalm 148:10.[47] Professor Jeffry H. Morrison has argued persuasively that the Declaration's references to "'divine Providence' and 'the Supreme Judge of the World' would have been quite acceptable to Reformed Americans in 1776, and conjured up images of the 'distinctly biblical God' when they heard or read the Declaration."[48] These terms for God may have been selected to appeal to a variety of Christian audiences, but there is little reason to believe they were used because the founders were deists.

It may be argued that Jefferson, the man who drafted the Declaration, was hardly an orthodox Christian. That is certainly the case, but this is beside the point. As Jefferson himself pointed out in his 1825 letter to Henry Lee, the object of the Declaration was not to "find out new principles, or new arguments . . . it was intended to be an expression of the American mind, and to give that expression the proper tone and spirit called for by the occasion. All its authority rests then on the harmonizing sentiments of the day."[49] Even though Jefferson may have believed in a vague, distant Deity, when his fellow delegates revised and approved the Declaration, virtually all of them understood that "Nature's God," "Creator," and "Providence" referred to the God of Abraham, Isaac, and Jacob—that is, a God who is active in the affairs of men and nations.

BUT FOR THE SAKE OF ARGUMENT . . .

Authors who contend that the founders were deists routinely highlight the views of some combination of eight men: Franklin, Washington, Adams, Jefferson, Madison, Hamilton, Allen, and Paine. If we accept a definition of deism that allows for God's intervention in human events (sometimes called "Providential Deism" or "theistic rationalism"), and ignore the lack of evidence that Washington, Madison, and Hamilton rejected orthodox Christianity, one might make a case that these founders were deists.[50] Yet, if these men were not representative of other founders, this finding suggests little with respect to the founding generation.

Consider for a moment the background and experiences of these founders. Washington, Jefferson, and Madison were southern Anglican plantation owners. Hamilton was born and raised in the British West Indies and, as an adult, along with Franklin, became a nominal Anglican. Paine was born and raised in England (he lived only twenty of his seventy-two years in America), and came from a Quaker background. In an era when few people traveled internationally, Jefferson and Adams spent significant time in Europe, and Franklin lived *most* of the last thirty-five years of his life in Britain and France. The only member of a Reformed church among these founders is Adams, but like some of his fellow Congregationalists (primarily in and around Boston), he moved rapidly toward Unitarianism.[51]

By way of contrast, in his magisterial history of religion in America, Sydney Ahlstrom observed that the Reformed tradition was "the religious heritage of three-fourths of the American people in 1776."[52] Similarly, Yale historian Harry Stout stated that, prior to the War of Independence, "the vast majority of colonists were Reformed or Calvinist."[53] These estimates may be high, but multiple studies demonstrate that Calvinist churches dominated New England and were well represented throughout the rest of the nation.[54] With the exception of John Adams, these Americans are unrepresented by the eight founders regularly discussed by those who contend the founders were deists. In social science lingo, these founders constitute an unrepresentative sample.

Adams was not the only member of a Reformed congregation to embrace something approximating deism in the founding era, but an excellent argument can be made that he is quite unrepresentative of civic leaders from the Reformed tradition. There is little reason to doubt, and much evidence to indicate, that the following Reformed founders were orthodox Christians: Samuel Adams, Elias Boudinot, Eliphalet Dyer, Oliver Ellsworth, Matthew Griswold, John Hancock, Benjamin Huntington, Samuel Huntington, Thomas McKean, William Paterson, Tapping Reeve, Jesse Root, Roger Sherman, John Treadwell, Jonathan Trumbull, William Williams, James Wilson, John Witherspoon, Oliver Wolcott, and Robert Yates.[55]

One might object that *these* twenty founders do not represent perfectly all of America's civic leaders, which is true. But they are better representatives of the 50–75 percent of Americans who are reasonably classified as Calvinists than the eight founders regularly called deists. If one were to focus on elite Anglicans, one would likely find more evidence of deism in the era, but (1) there were not many elite Anglicans in America, and (2) one would find pious and orthodox men, including John Jay, Patrick Henry, and Henry Laurens, in this group. Because some founders did not leave many letters, diaries, or other documents that shed light on their religious convictions, it is often difficult to discern much more than which church a particular founder attended and/or joined. But students of the founding era should be careful not to read too much into this lack of evidence—and they certainly should not extrapolate from the absence of texts to the conclusion that these founders embraced deism. And it is obviously bad social science *and* bad history to generalize the views of the founders as a whole from the views of a few unrepresentative elites.

For evidence that the examples of "orthodox" founders listed above were, in fact, orthodox Christians, please refer to the "Suggestions for Further Reading" at the end of this chapter. There are good reasons to believe that many of America's founders were orthodox Christians, and there is virtually no evidence to suggest that most (or even many) of them were deists, at least as that term is popularly and historically understood. Scholars and activists who contend that "most of the American founders embraced some form of Deism, not historically orthodox Christianity,"[56] should either find additional evidence to support such assertions or show that Franklin, Washington, Adams, Jefferson, Madison, Hamilton, Allen, and Paine represent the religious views of their fellow founders. If they cannot, they should limit their claims to these men. And, if they are careful, they should, in the absence of more compelling evidence, remove Washington, Madison, and Hamilton from their lists of founders who were deists. Moreover, if by "deism" they include the idea that God is a "Creator or First Cause who subsequently stood aside from his creation to allow it to run according to its own rules,"[57] they must acknowledge that the number of civic leaders in the founding era who were deists may be only one—Ethan Allen.

SUGGESTIONS FOR FURTHER READING

Dreisbach, Daniel L. *Reading the Bible with the Founding Fathers*. New York: Oxford University Press, 2017. Demonstrates that the Bible had a tremendous influence in the founding era.

Dreisbach, Daniel L., Mark D. Hall, and Jeffry H. Morrison, eds. *The Founders on God and Government*. Lanham: Rowman & Littlefield, 2004. Contains profiles of George Washington, John Adams, Thomas Jefferson, James Madison, John Witherspoon, Benjamin Franklin, James Wilson, George Mason, and the Carrolls of Maryland.

Dreisbach, Daniel L., Mark David Hall, and Jeffry H. Morrison, eds. *The Forgotten Founders on Religion and Public Life*. Notre Dame: University of Notre Dame Press, 2009. Includes profiles of Abigail

Adams, Samuel Adams, Oliver Ellsworth, Alexander Hamilton, Patrick Henry, John Jay, Thomas Paine, Edmund Randolph, Benjamin Rush, Roger Sherman, and Mercy Otis Warren.

Dreisbach, Daniel L., and Mark David Hall, eds. *Faith and the Founders of the American Republic*. New York: Oxford University Press, 2014. Offers profiles of Gouverneur Morris, John Hancock, Elias Boudinot, John Dickinson, and Isaac Backus. Also includes eight thematic chapters on topics including deism, Judaism, and Islam.

Kidd, Thomas S. *God of Liberty: A Religious History of the American Revolution*. New York: Basic Books, 2010. A superb account of the important role Christianity played in America's founding.

Richard, Carl J. *The Founders and the Bible*. Lanham: Rowman & Littlefield, 2016. Helps demonstrate that many founders were orthodox Christians who had a high view of the Bible.

CHAPTER 2

THE UNITED STATES DOES NOT HAVE A GODLESS CONSTITUTION

The U.S. Constitution, drafted in 1787 and
ratified in 1788, is a godless document.
ISAAC KRAMNICK AND R. LAURENCE MOORE,
THE GODLESS CONSTITUTION

The Constitution . . . essentially created a secular state. Nowhere
does the Constitution mention God or any other religious symbol.
RICHARD HUGHES, MYTHS AMERICA LIVES BY

The omission of one word—God—played an even more important role
in the construction of a secular Foundation for the new government.
SUSAN JACOBY, FREETHINKERS: A HISTORY OF AMERICAN SECULARISM

In 1787, within the whole of Western political culture, the secularity of
the Constitution of the United States was indeed an isolated anomaly.
DEREK DAVIS, RELIGION AND THE CONTINENTAL CONGRESS

The founders "created the first wholly secular state."
JOSEPH J. ELLIS, AMERICAN CREATION[1]

Scholars and popular writers regularly assert that the US Constitution is a secular or even "godless" document. If by this they mean simply that God is not featured prominently in the text of the Constitution, they may have a point—albeit a trivial one. Unlike some public documents of the day, the Constitution does not, for all intents and purposes, mention God. By way of contrast, the nation's first constitution, the Articles of Confederation (1781), invokes the "great Governor of the universe."[2] Similarly, many state constitutions of the era contain references to God and Christianity. Consider, for instance, the Massachusetts Constitution of 1780:

> We, therefore, the people of Massachusetts, acknowledging, with grateful hearts, the goodness of the great Legislator of the universe, in affording us, in the course of His providence, an opportunity, deliberately and peaceably, without fraud, violence, or surprise, of entering into an original, explicit, and solemn compact with each other, and of forming a new constitution of civil government, for ourselves and posterity; and devoutly imploring His direction in so interesting a design, do agree upon, ordain, and establish, the following *Declaration of Rights, and Frame of Government*, as the CONSTITUTION OF

THE COMMONWEALTH OF MASSACHUSETTS.[3] (emphasis original)

Similar examples can be given from other state constitutions, which highlight the absence of such statements from the US Constitution. Many writers have made much of this absence. But do these arguments stand up to scrutiny?

"In the Year of Our Lord" and Christian Practices

God is not completely absent from the Constitution. Article VII proclaims that the document was framed *"in the year of our Lord* one thousand seven hundred and eighty seven and of the Independence of the United States of America the twelfth"[4] (emphasis added). Jasper Adams, a nineteenth-century minister, president of the College of Charleston, and scion of the famous Adams family, contended that this phrase constitutes "a distinct recognition of the authority of Christ, and, of course, of his religion by the people of the United States."[5] Similarly, B. F. Morris observed that Article VII "affirms [the Constitution's] Christian character and purpose."[6]

If America's founders desired to create a thoroughly secular political order, they might have avoided the convention "in the year of our Lord" altogether. The radicals of the French Revolution, for instance, did not mention the Deity in their famous Declaration of the Rights of Man, and they went so far as to adopt a new calendar based on the "autumnal equinox, the day after their republic was proclaimed," rather than rely on the traditional designation of AD (*Anno Domini*—"In the year of our Lord").[7]

Members of the Convention did not insert the phrase "in the year of our Lord" into the Constitution; it was added by the scribe who penned the final version of the document.[8] But it *was* in the text signed by thirty-nine of the delegates to the Federal Convention (not all fifty-five delegates signed the Constitution) and ratified by state conventions. It is not unreasonable to cite Article VII as evidence that the Constitution is not godless, but because documents in the era were routinely dated "in the year of our Lord," it is best not to rely too heavily on this argument.[9]

If the Constitution does not refer to God prominently, it does assume some Christian practices. The fourth commandment admonishes believers to "remember the Sabbath day, to keep it holy" (Ex. 20:8). States and localities regularly prohibited work on Sunday,[10] and the Constitutional Convention met every day of the week *except* for the Christian Sabbath.[11] The Constitution itself assumes that Congress will not conduct business on that day; Article I stipulates that "any bill not returned by the president within ten Days (Sundays excepted) . . . shall be a law."[12] Congress is not formally prohibited from convening on the Lord's Day, but prior to the twentieth century, the House of Representatives did so only on one occasion.[13] Members of the federal government did meet in the US Capitol on Sunday, but as we shall see in chapter 3, they did so for worship services.

The unamended Constitution contains three oath requirements, and most founders could not conceive of oaths in anything other than religious terms.[14] In Connecticut's ratifying convention, for instance, Oliver Wolcott observed that the "Constitution enjoins an oath upon all the officers of the United States. This is a direct appeal to God, who is the avenger of perjury."[15] Similarly, future Supreme Court Justice James Iredell of North Carolina remarked in his state's ratifying convention that according "to the modern definition of an oath, it is considered 'a solemn appeal to the

Supreme Being . . . and in a future state of rewards and punishments.'"[16] Americans have shifted away from understanding oaths as essentially religious exercises, but most founders thought otherwise.[17]

On its face, the Constitution is not completely godless, and it assumes some Christian practice. But there are far more substantial reasons for rejecting the proposition that America has a godless Constitution. Before turning to those reasons, we should consider founders who *were* troubled by the absence of an explicit acknowledgment of God in the Constitution.

Amending the Constitution for Christ?

Connecticut's William Williams, a signer of the Declaration and member of Connecticut's ratification convention, believed that it was a mistake to not overtly acknowledge the Deity in the nation's fundamental law. He proposed to remedy this defect by amending the Constitution to begin:

> We the people of the United States, in a firm belief of the being and perfections of the one living and true God, the creator and supreme Governor of the world, in His universal providence and the authority of His laws; that He will require of all moral agents an account of their conduct, that all rightful powers among men are ordained of, and mediately derived from God; therefore in a dependence on His blessing and acknowledgment of his efficient protection in establishing our Independence, whereby it is become necessary to agree upon and settle a Constitution of federal government for ourselves, and in order to form a more perfect union &c . . .[18]

The Constitution's lack of references to God bothered others as well, and objectors continued to agitate for a constitutional amendment, similar to that proposed by Williams, well into the nineteenth century.[19] Yet many indisputably pious founders had no qualms about supporting the Constitution without such language.[20] In the midst of the ratification debates, the pseudonymous "Elihu" responded in a newspaper essay to Williams's proposal, arguing that:

> [God was not] like a foolish old man, [who] will think himself slighted and dishonored if he is not complimented with a seat or a prologue of recognition in the Constitution. . . . [Instead,] those great philosophers who formed the Constitution had a higher idea of the perfection of that INFINITE MIND which governs all worlds than to suppose they could add to his honor or glory, or that he would be pleased with such low familiarity or vulgar flattery.[21]

Elihu's argument is persuasive, but the major reason Federalists opposed Williams's amendment was that they opposed *all* amendments during the ratification debates. They recognized that any attempt to revise the Constitution before it was ratified would significantly slow ratification, if it didn't kill the Constitution altogether. Hence, they opposed all amendments, even those aimed at protecting rights every founder agreed were fundamental, such as freedom of religion, speech, and the press.[22]

With the exception of the Constitution being dated "in the year of our Lord," those who believe that America has a godless constitution are correct that God is not referenced in the document. If this were their only point, they could make it in a sentence rather than in books. But they do have more to say. To support their thesis, they rely on two substantive arguments: first, that "many" or "most" of the founders were deists (a claim I have already shown to be demonstrably false); and second, that the Constitution's framers were influenced by rationalist, Enlightenment ideas.[23] In the remainder of this chapter, I show that this second claim is overstated and misleading, and contend instead that the founders drew heavily from Christian ideas when they crafted America's constitutional order.

To Whom Did the Founders Turn?

Matthew Stewart, in his book *Nature's God: The Heretical Origins of the American Republic*, contends that Benedict de Spinoza, a seventeenth-century rationalist, is the "principal architect of the radical political philosophy that achieves its ultimate expression in the American republic, and Locke is its acceptable face."[24] That Americans learned of Spinoza through John Locke is a necessary concession for Stewart, as even he admits that "there was—and is—no meaningful evidence at all in revolutionary America of Spinoza's influence."[25] I wish I could report that Stewart made this outlandish claim in an obscure and self-published book, but *Nature's God* was released by a major publisher to a great deal of critical acclaim.[26]

Stewart's book is pure fantasy. More plausible is the contention that America's founders were influenced by Enlightenment thinkers such as John Locke, the Baron of Montesquieu, Jean-Jacques Rousseau, and Adam Smith.[27] Particularly significant, scholars and popular authors contend, was a secularized version of Locke's political ideas. The influential historian Carl L. Becker, for instance, asserted that revolutionary era Americans "had absorbed Locke's works as a kind of political gospel."[28] More recently, Isaac Kramnick and R. Laurence Moore contend that Locke's writings "most shaped the intellectual and political world view of Americans in the eighteenth century." And political scientist Barbara McGraw claims that "Lockean fundamentals . . . shaped the conscience of the American Founders" with respect to the role of religion in public life.[29]

If these and other scholars are correct, one would expect to see Locke's *Second Treatise* everywhere in early America. Yet, with very few exceptions, Locke's works were not available on this side of the Atlantic until 1714, when bulky three-volume editions of his writings began appearing in university libraries.[30] The *Second Treatise* was not published in America until 1773, and it was not republished in the United States until 1937.[31]

By the 1760s and 1770s, American patriots cited Locke with some regularity to support American resistance to Great Britain. Yet, as Donald S. Lutz has shown, the Bible was referenced far more often than his works. In his extraordinary study of American political literature published between 1760 and 1805, Lutz found that 22 percent of the citations referenced Enlightenment thinkers (a list that includes Montesquieu, Locke, Pufendorf, Hume, Hobbes, and Beccaria, among others). By contrast, 34 percent of all citations were to the Bible. Only 2.9 percent of the citations to individual authors were to Locke. For our purposes, it is important to note that Lutz *undercounted* references to the Bible because he excluded from his sample political sermons that do not cite secular authors. If he had included these sermons, references to the Bible would have absolutely dwarfed any other grouping of texts.[32]

If Locke's works were late to arrive on America's shores, the Bible was virtually omnipresent from the first days of the Puritan settlements. The fine American historian Joyce Appleby observed that the "most important source of meaning for eighteenth-century Americans was the Bible."[33] Daniel L. Dreisbach has recently provided extensive documentation demonstrating that the Bible was the most influential book in the founding era.[34] Many founders continued to look to it for guidance, and virtually all of them referred to it regularly in their public and private speeches and writings. This reality is often overlooked because the founders assumed their audiences were familiar with God's Word and so did not include textual citations. As Benjamin Franklin explained to Samuel Cooper in 1781:

> It was not necessary in New England, where everybody reads the Bible, and is acquainted with Scripture phrases, that you should note the texts from which you took them; but I have observed in England, as well as in France, that verses and expressions taken from the sacred writings and not known to be such, appear very strange and awkward to some readers; and I shall therefore in my edition take the liberty of marking the quoted texts in the margin.[35]

The Holy Scriptures were the most important source of authority for America's founders, but they are not a handbook for politics. So when the founders debated the War of Independence, the creation of a new state and national constitutions, and the proper scope of liberty to be protected by governments, they turned to thinkers such as Locke and Montesquieu for guidance. They saw these authors as articulating ideas that were compatible with their Christian convictions.

In the final analysis, the question of whether America has a godly or godless Constitution cannot be answered by counting the number of references to God and the Bible in its text or in the political literature of the era. Instead, it is necessary to consider the ideas that influenced the civic leaders who drafted and ratified the document. When one does so, it becomes clear that Christian commitments played an influential—even dominant—role in the drafting and ratification of the Constitution.

THE FOUNDERS' SYLLOGISM

Before considering the Constitution per se, let's explore a more abstract, but essential, conviction of the founders that makes self-government possible. With few, if any, exceptions, every founding-era statesman was committed to the proposition that republican government required a moral citizenry, and that religion was necessary for morality. James Hutson of the Library of Congress suggests that this argument was so widespread that it should be called the "Founding generation's syllogism."[36] When America's founders spoke about "religion," virtually all of them—even those most influenced by the Enlightenment—meant Christianity. The great Chief Justice John Marshall wrote, for example, that in America "Christianity and religion are identified. It would be strange, indeed, if with such a people, our institutions did not presuppose Christianity."[37]

The exception that proves this rule is a 1789 letter by Benjamin Rush, in which he contended that the "only Foundation for a useful education in a republic is to be laid in religion. Without this there can be no virtue, and without virtue there can be no liberty, and liberty is the object and life of all republican governments." With a liberality unusual in his generation, he continued,

Such is my veneration for every religion that reveals the attributes of the Deity, or a future state of rewards and punishments, that I had rather see the opinions of Confucius or Mahomed inculcated upon our youth, than see them grow up wholly devoid of a system of religious principles. But the religion I mean to recommend in this place, is that of the New Testament.[38]

Rush ended where many founders began, with the default assumption that Christianity supported and promoted virtues that allow republican government to flourish. His suggestion that other religions foster the moral commitments necessary for republicanism, while intriguing, seems to have been primarily a thought experiment.

Shortly before America declared independence, John Adams wrote that "Religion and morality alone . . . can establish the principles upon which freedom can securely stand."[39] He regularly reiterated this conviction, noting in 1811, for instance, that "religion and virtue are the only Foundations, not only of republicanism and of all free government, but of social felicity under all governments and in all combinations of human society."[40] Referring specifically to the US Constitution, he wrote in 1798 that "our constitution was made only for a moral and religious people. It is wholly inadequate to the government of any other."[41]

Among other benefits, religion and virtue help create a unified, safe, and peaceful society. In the words of Elizur Goodrich, a Congregationalist minister from Connecticut, "religion and virtue are the strongest bond of human society, and lay the best foundation of peace and happiness in the civil state."[42] In 1796, future Supreme Court Justice Samuel Chase wrote in a Maryland General Court opinion that "religion is of general and public concern, and on its support depend, in great measure, the peace and good order of government, the safety and happiness of the people."[43] Similarly, Jedidiah Morse, a Congregationalist minister, figurative "father of American geography," and actual father of Samuel F. B. Morse (inventor of the telegraph), preached an election sermon in 1799 where he observed that it is to

> the kindly influence of Christianity we owe that degree of civil freedom, and political and social happiness which mankind now enjoys. . . . All efforts to destroy the Foundation of our holy religion, ultimately tend to the subversion also of our political freedom and happiness. Whenever the pillars of Christianity shall be overthrown, our present republican form of government, and all the blessings which flow from them, must fall with them.[44]

Such sentiments were not limited to Protestants. Charles Carroll of Maryland, a Roman Catholic signer of the Declaration of Independence, remarked that "without morals a republic cannot subsist any length of time; they therefore who are decrying the Christian religion, whose morality is so sublime & pure . . . are undermining the solid Foundation of morals, the best security for the duration of a free government."[45]

Few founders were more insistent on the importance of religion and morality than George Washington. For instance, in his 1783 "Circular Letter to the States," written upon his resignation as commander-in-chief of the Continental army, he concluded with an "earnest prayer" that God

> would most graciously be pleased to dispose us all, to do justice, to love mercy, and to demean ourselves with that charity, humility, and pacific temper of mind, which were the characteristics of the Divine Author of our blessed religion, and without a humble imitation of whose example in these things, we can never hope to be a happy nation.[46]

This brief prayer includes a paraphrase of Micah 6:8, one of Washington's favorite verses, which admonished people "to do justly, and to love mercy, and to walk humbly" with God.[47] Note his strong claim that America can "*never* hope to be a happy nation" unless it imitates the characteristics of "the Divine Author of our blessed religion" (Jesus Christ), such as "charity, humility, and pacific temper of mind." National happiness is intimately connected with these virtues.

CONTEXT MATTERS

Historians such as John Fea emphasize the importance of "context,"[48] but in their rush to deny that America had a Christian founding, they often ignore it. So, for instance, Fea claims that Washington's circular is not a "uniquely 'Christian' document."[49] But there is no reason to think that anybody understood Washington as encouraging his readers to imitate the characteristics of anyone other than God's Son Jesus Christ— for to whom else could "*Divine* Author of our blessed religion" refer?[50] (emphasis added). Certainly, someone could call a non-Christian deity "Divine Author," "Providence," or "Father," but to apply Fea's logic to the Lord's Prayer, which begins "Our Father who art in heaven," and conclude that it is not "uniquely 'Christian'" would be, at best, misleading.[51]

As the end of his service as president drew near, Washington published an essay commonly referred to as his "Farewell Address."[52]

In it, he returned to the importance of religion and morality for the nation, noting:

> Of all the dispositions and habits which lead to political prosperity, religion and morality are indisputable supports. In vain would that man claim the tribute of patriotism, who should labor to subvert these great pillars of human happiness, these firmest props of the duty of men and citizens. . . . A volume could not trace all their connections with private and public felicity. Let it simply be asked where is the security for property, for reputation, for life, if the sense of religious obligation *desert* the oaths, which are the instruments of investigation in courts of justice? And let us with caution indulge the supposition, that morality can be maintained without religion. Whatever may be conceded to the influence of refined education on minds of peculiar structure, reason and experience both forbid us to expect that national morality can prevail in exclusion of religious principle.[53] (emphasis original)

Washington emphasized that religion and morality, in addition to being necessary for personal and public happiness, are essential for ensuring the sanctity of oaths. Like many founders, he thought that belief in God and an afterlife, where one's deeds would be punished or rewarded, was necessary to ensure that people tell "the truth, the whole truth, and nothing but the truth, *so help me God*"[54] (emphasis original). He acknowledged that a few individuals could be moral without being religious, but he clearly thought these were exceptions to the general rule. "National morality" requires religion, and Washington went so far as to question the patriotism of those who "labor to subvert these great pillars of human happiness."

Examples of founders insisting that religion is necessary for morality, and that both religion and morality are necessary for republican government, could be multiplied almost indefinitely. The logic is compelling. If republican government is to work, people need to respect one another. This includes engaging in political debate with civility, treating one's opponents with dignity, telling the truth, and the like. More important, religion is a source of internal control, restraining and disciplining each citizen, and thus limiting the need for external control by civil government. A religious and, therefore, a moral citizenry is necessary before statesmen can even begin to think about constitutional systems.[55]

HUMAN NATURE: FEDERALISM, SEPARATION OF POWERS, AND CHECKS AND BALANCES

The ancient Greek philosopher Plato argued in *The Republic* that a society can be just only if virtuous philosophers are put in charge, because they alone are capable of knowing justice. So if a country desires just laws and policies, it follows that philosophers must rule. Plato had an optimistic view of human nature. He believed that if these philosophers were educated properly they would rule justly, with no checks on their power, for a very long time. But even he recognized that they would eventually fall prey to corruption.[56]

In the eighteenth century, utopian views of another sort began to arise. Rather than rely on the rule of a virtuous elite, some thinkers began to suggest that the elites were, in fact, the problem. They argued that political power should be turned over to the virtuous yeoman, especially farmers living in communion with nature, who could be trusted to create laws that advance the common good. The most famous proponent of this view was the Genevan-born philosopher Jean-Jacques Rousseau.[57] Influenced by these sorts of ideas, Tom Paine promoted unicameral legislatures with few checks and balances other than annual elections.[58] He believed this structure would best allow the will of the people to be transformed into just laws. Pennsylvania adopted such a system in 1776, but this experiment was clearly a failure and was abandoned in 1790.[59]

Fortunately, few American founders were drawn into either type of utopian speculation. This is because their faith taught them that "all have sinned, and come short of the glory of God" (Rom. 3:23). Moreover, they recognized that Christians continue to struggle with sin. So even if elected officials are persons of faith, citizens must still be wary of political corruption. Like Lord Acton, they were convinced that "power tends to corrupt, and absolute power corrupts absolutely."[60]

All orthodox Christians believe that humans are sinful, but they disagree about the impact sin has on them. Calvinists are famous for emphasizing the corrosive effects of the Fall. They commonly insist that humans are "totally depraved," and that the unredeemed are able to turn to God only because of His irresistible grace. And they, more than many other believers, insist that even saints continue to struggle with sin. This is particularly relevant in America, because Calvinism was "the religious heritage of three-fourths of the American people in 1776."[61]

Not only were most Americans in the founding era Calvinists, Reformed citizens exercised significant influence through a variety of venues. Literally, millions of children were taught to read with the Calvinist *New-England Primer*. More than two million copies of this reader were printed in the eighteenth century alone, and in spite of its name, the text was used throughout America. Innumerable children learned the alphabet with a rhyme that began: "In *Adam's* Fall, We sinned all."[62]

Many teachers in this era were Calvinists. For instance, James Madison was educated by the Scottish Presbyterian minister Donald Robertson (about whom he later said, "all that I have been in life I owe largely to that man"), the Anglican rector Thomas Martin (a graduate of the Presbyterian College of New Jersey), and the Presbyterian minister John Witherspoon.[63] When Witherspoon was president of the College of New Jersey (now Princeton), the school produced "five delegates to the Constitutional Convention, one US President (Madison), a vice president (the notorious Aaron Burr), forty-nine US representatives, twenty-eight US senators, three Supreme Court justices, eight US district judges, one secretary of state, three attorneys general, and two foreign ministers."[64]

Given this background, it should come as no surprise that the delegates who gathered in Philadelphia in 1787 were not utopian theorists presuming the best about human nature. Throughout the Convention debates, they frequently worried that political leaders might become corrupt or tyrannical.[65] Such fears led Madison, who had drafted a proposed constitution now known as the Virginia Plan, to suggest a bristling array of checks and balances. His plan included a legislature where members of the lower house would be elected by the people from proportionately sized districts; there would be an upper house, whose members would be chosen by the lower house from candidates nominated by state legislatures; an executive and judges would be appointed by the legislature, and acting together, they could negate legislation; and the national legislature would have a general grant of power and the ability to veto state laws.[66]

The Virginia Plan was far from utopian, but other delegates objected that it concentrated too much power in the national government. Roger Sherman, a latter-day Puritan from Connecticut, favored strengthening the national government, but only for a few limited ends.

The objects of the Union, he thought were few. 1. defense against foreign danger. 2. against internal disputes & a resort to force. 3. treaties with foreign nations. 4. regulating foreign commerce, & drawing revenue from it. . . . All other matters civil & criminal would be much better in the hands of the states.[67]

Sherman and like-minded delegates eventually won this debate, which resulted in Article I, Section 8, of the Constitution. This section limits the national government to doing things that really must be done by a national government, such as negotiating treaties, declaring war, and regulating commerce between (but not within) the states. All other matters, to the extent to which they should be addressed by governments at all, are the responsibility of state and local bodies.

The founders thought that limiting the power of the national government was necessary but not sufficient to prevent corruption and tyranny. They were committed to separating power between the legislative, executive, and judicial branches. They believed as well that each branch must have the ability to check the other. For instance, a president may veto legislation he considers to be unconstitutional or imprudent, or that infringes upon his authority. Federal courts, likewise, may declare void legislation that judges believe to be unconstitutional or unjust (discussed below). The founders understood that this complicated system would make it difficult to pass legislation, but they considered this cost to be well worth the benefit of protecting and preserving liberty.

In the Constitutional Convention and ratifying debates, the founders referenced with some regularity Montesquieu's 1748 work, *The Spirit of the Laws.*[68] In this book, Montesquieu attempted to understand how power was separated in Great Britain's political institutions, and how each branch checked the other. Although he got some details wrong, this treatise helped convince later civic leaders, especially those in America, of the importance of the separation of powers and checks and balances. Indeed, Donald Lutz's previously mentioned study found that 8.3 percent of all citations to individual authors were to Montesquieu.[69]

Although Montesquieu is fairly characterized as an Enlightenment thinker, the founders were drawn to him because he addressed a dilemma that all Christian statesmen must face: government is a necessary, God-ordained institution (Rom. 13), but even the best rulers are sinful. Because power tends to corrupt, the pressing question was how to design political institutions that make it less likely that rulers will succumb to vice, and that limit the damage they can do if they do. Early American colonial governments separated power to some degree, and many attempted to limit the power of rulers in other ways, but Montesquieu offered new insights into the ways in which separation of powers and checks and balances could help prevent tyranny.

America's founders did not follow Montesquieu blindly, nor did they always agree with each other. The Presbyterian James Wilson, for instance, thought that the president should have far more power than did the Congregationalist Roger Sherman. Some Christians fought against the adoption of the Constitution because they believed it did not limit the national government's power enough. My argument that the founders were influenced by their Christian commitments doesn't mean they always came to the same conclusions. But they did regularly agree on foundational Christian principles, such as the reality that humans are sinful and that power tends to corrupt.

James Madison's view of human nature was similar to that held by Calvinists.[70] In *Federalist* No. 49, he specifically rejected Plato's idea of philosopher-kings, noting that "in a nation of philosophers . . . [a]

reverence for the laws would be sufficiently inculcated by the voice of an enlightened reason. But a nation of philosophers is as little to be expected as the philosophical race of kings wished for by Plato."[71] In *Federalist* No. 51, he went on to observe that "if men were angels, no government would be necessary. If angels were to govern men, neither external or internal controls on government would be necessary."[72] The essay then explains that the separation of powers, checks and balances, and federalism are necessary to prevent corruption and promote justice.

In light of the broad and sweeping consensus among America's founders that humans are sinful and that concentrated power should be avoided, it is surprising that so many academics continue to assert that the founders were primarily influenced by Enlightenment thought.[73] By the late eighteenth century, European Enlightenment thinkers such as Nicolas de Condorcet were "well on their way to envisioning a benign human nature and even a perfectible one free of original sin."[74] Practically, this led them to reject the separation of powers, checks and balances, and federalism. According to Barry Alan Shain, one of the best students of religion in the American founding, "by the 1770s, most leading Enlightenment thinkers embraced unicameralism" and many "leading lights of the Enlightenment" ridiculed American feder-alism.[75] There were a few short-lived experiments with unicameralism in post-Revolutionary America, but most founders knew better. In the words of Louis Hartz, America's founders "refused to join in the great Enlightenment enterprise of shattering the Christian concept of sin, replacing it with an unlimited humanism, and then emerging with an earthly paradise as glittering as the heavenly one that had been destroyed."[76] This explains in large part why the constitutional order created in 1787 has been so successful, whereas that created by the leaders of the French Revolution ended in disaster.

NATURAL LAW AND NATURAL RIGHTS: BILLS OF RIGHTS

Scholars have spilled a great deal of ink debating the origins of the idea that individuals have rights that governments may not violate. The medievalist Brian Tierney has argued that a sophisticated understanding of natural rights based on a Christian conception of natural law was being articulated as early as the twelfth century.[77] John Witte Jr. of Emory University contends in his magisterial *The Reformation of Rights: Law, Religion, and Morality in Early Modern Calvinism* that Protestantism played a key role in the development of the idea of individual rights.[78] By the late eighteenth century, most Americans were committed to the ideas, as expressed in the Declaration of Independence, that "all men are created equal; that they are endowed by their Creator with certain unalienable rights; that among these are life, liberty, and the pursuit of happiness."

America's founders regularly appealed to natural law and natural rights, but they seldom addressed these subjects in a systematic manner. The most prominent exception to this rule is found in James Wilson's 1790–1792 law lectures at the College of Philadelphia. Born in Scotland and educated at the University of Saint Andrews, Wilson immigrated to America in 1765, and quickly became an influential attorney. A signer of the Declaration of Independence and an important nationalist at the Constitutional Convention, Wilson was one of Washington's first appointments to the US Supreme Court. He served on the court until his death in 1798.

In his law lectures, Wilson sounded like Saint Thomas Aquinas when he observed that there are two types of law: divine and human. Wilson went on to explain that there are four "species" of divine law: eternal, celestial, natural physical, and natural moral. Like Aquinas, he thought that human law "must rest its authority, ultimately, upon the authority of that law which is divine."[79] Practically, this led him (and all but one Supreme Court justice prior to John Marshall) to publicly assert that the Supreme Court could strike down an act of Congress if it violated *natural law*.[80]

Wilson followed Aquinas in many respects, but unlike him, he offered a rich account of the natural rights possessed by individuals.[81] He argued that because natural rights are based on natural law, they exist prior to government. And protecting these rights is among the government's most important responsibilities. He asked rhetorically,

> What was the primary and principal object in the institution of government? Was it—I speak of the primary and principal object— was it to acquire new rights by a human establishment? Or was it, by a human establishment, to acquire a new security for the possession or the recovery of those rights, to the enjoyment or acquisition of which we were previously entitled by the immediate gift, or by the unerring law, of our all-wise and all-beneficent Creator? The latter, I presume, was the case.[82]

The idea that governments should respect and protect individual natural rights was not invented by America's founders. This belief was central to the Christian—especially Protestant—conviction that tyrants may be actively resisted by either inferior magistrates or the people themselves.[83] Some Christians held (and hold) that this view is incompatible with Romans 13, which seems on the surface to require Christians to obey even evil rulers. But from the mid-sixteenth century forward, many Protestant political thinkers, including the vast majority of America's founders, rejected this idea and agreed that the Bible permits, or even requires, citizens to actively resist tyrants. This doctrine is important if we are to understand why the American War of Independence was a just war.[84] But here I want to suggest that the founders' belief in natural rights informed another important aspect of American constitutionalism: bills of rights.

A commitment to individual rights *and* the belief that rulers are sinful and fallible naturally leads to the question of how one's rights can be protected against political authorities. We have already seen several answers to this problem, including fostering a virtuous citizenry, federalism, separation of powers, and checks and balances. Another important protection is a statutory or constitutional delineation of rights that may not be infringed by governments. New England Puritans adopted such practices as early as the mid-seventeenth century. Massachusetts Bay's 1641 Body of Liberties contains many protections later found in the US Bill of Rights, including prohibitions against double jeopardy, torture, and "in-humane barbarous or cruel" bodily punishments.[85] Seven years later, these laws were revised and published as *The Book of the General Lawes and Libertyes Concerning the Inhabitants of Massachusetts.* According to David D. Hall of Harvard's Divinity School, this is the first time a legal code had ever been printed in the Western world—an innovation that made it possible to distribute the laws more widely than if they were copied by hand.[86]

When the colonies broke from Great Britain, many of the newly independent states created bills of rights to ensure that state governments did not infringe upon the natural rights of citizens. The new national Constitution of 1787 did not include a bill of rights because the federal government was one of strictly limited powers. The Federalists argued that Congress had no power to restrain the press or prohibit the free exercise of religion, so adding a bill of rights to prevent it from taking these measures would have been superfluous. But the Anti-Federalists were not convinced and insisted on adding one. The First Federal Congress agreed, proposing twelve amendments to the Constitution. Ten of these were ratified in the eighteenth century, and they are today collectively known as the Bill of Rights.

One does not need to be a Christian to appreciate the value of natural rights or limited government. But in the American context, it is clear that the founders valued them, at least in part, for theological reasons. It is true that some judicial or procedural rights, such as the right to trial by jury, were drawn from other sources. America's founders were influenced by the British common law tradition, although this tradition itself was heavily informed by Christianity (see, for instance, Supreme Court Justice Joseph Story's 1833 essay "Christianity a Part of the Common Law").[87] We cannot explore every natural right valued by the founders here, but a brief consideration of the founders' understanding of the rights to life and liberty helps show how their view differs from that embraced by too many citizens and judges today.

THE RIGHT TO LIFE

America's founders did not have a utopian view of human nature, but they did have a high view of it. This is because they were committed to the core Christian idea that all humans are created in the *imago Dei* (image of God), which means, in part, that men and women are reasonable, creative beings. This led the founders to conclude that "we the people" (as opposed to the elite) can order our public lives together through politics rather than force.

It also informed their view of rights. In his Supreme Court opinion in *Chisholm v. Georgia* (1793), Justice James Wilson, paraphrasing

Psalm 139, observed that "man, fearfully and wonderfully made, is the workmanship of his all perfect Creator."[88] He echoed this conviction in his law lectures.[89] One practical implication of this is that innocent life must always be protected. Wilson wrote with evident approval,

> With consistency, beautiful and undeviating, human life, from its commencement to its close, is protected by the common law. In the contemplation of law, life begins when the infant is first able to stir in the womb. By the law, life is protected not only from immediate destruction, but from every degree of actual violence, and, in some cases, from every degree of danger.[90]

Based on this principle, Wilson criticized ancient societies, such as Sparta, Athens, China, and Rome, for the practice of exposing or killing unwanted infants.[91] He also condemned the "gentle Hindoo" who "is laudably averse to the shedding of blood; but he carries his worn out friend and benefactor to perish on the banks of the Ganges."[92] And, like most Christian legal theorists, he condemned suicide because

> it was not by his own voluntary act that the man made his appearance upon the theatre of life; he cannot, therefore, plead the right of the nation, by his own voluntary act to make his exit. He did not make; therefore, he has no right to destroy himself. He alone, whose gift this state of existence is, has the right to say when and how it shall receive its termination.[93]

Wilson supported the death penalty for crimes such as murder and treason. If a person is sentenced to death, however, he stipulated in a grand jury charge that "an interval should be permitted to elapse before its execution, as will render the language of political expediency consonant to the language of religion."[94]

BLACKSTONE AND THE RIGHT TO LIFE

William Blackstone's four-volume *Commentaries on the Laws of England* (1765–1769) had a significant influence on late eighteenth-century American law. Wilson and other founders disagreed with him on some important issues, such as natural rights and parliamentary supremacy, but they all agreed that unborn babies are protected by law. Early in the first volume of this work, Blackstone wrote,

> Life is the immediate gift of God, a right inherent by nature in every individual; and it begins in contemplation of law as soon as an infant is able to stir in the mother's womb. For if a woman is quick with child, and by a potion, or otherwise, kills it in her womb; or if any one beat her, whereby the child dies in her body, and she is delivered of a dead child; this, though not murder, was by the ancient law homicide or manslaughter.[95]

The founders' conviction that humans are created in the image of God and that innocent lives should be protected calls into question Supreme Court precedents such as *Roe v. Wade*, 410 U.S. 113 (1973), where justices discovered a right to have an abortion hiding in a previously undiscovered "right to privacy," tucked away among the Bill of Rights' "penumbras" and "emanations."[96] At a minimum, an originalist understanding of the Bill of Rights would require the Supreme Court to overturn *Roe* and return the issue of abortion to the states. And if state legislators share the founders' conviction that all humans are created in the image of God, they would ban the practice in all but the most rare and extreme cases.[97]

That all humans are created in the image of God logically suggests that one person should not own another. Many founders were coming to this conclusion, although self-interest undoubtedly made it difficult for many slave owners to accept this conclusion. For instance, in one remarkable case, slavery led John Rutledge of South Carolina to reject the almost universal consensus that religion and morality should inform public policy. When slavery was debated in the Constitutional Convention, he contended that "religion & humanity had nothing to do with this question—interest alone is the governing principle with nations—the true question at present is whether the Southern states shall or shall not be parties to the Union."[98] Few founders echoed Rutledge's relentlessly amoral approach to slavery. Due to space, I cannot discuss the founders' approach to slavery here. For now, it is sufficient to say that many of them were coming to question the legitimacy of the practice because of, not despite, their Christian convictions.[99]

"PROCLAIM LIBERTY THROUGHOUT ALL THE LAND . . ."

Liberty is a core American value. The War of Independence was fought, in large measure, to protect political and religious liberty. Patriots adopted a variety of symbols to demonstrate their love of freedom, from liberty trees to liberty caps to the famous Liberty Bell. Daniel L. Dreisbach shows that civic and religious leaders alike regularly appealed to Scripture to support their arguments for liberty. Galatians 5:1 was the most cited verse in this respect: "Stand fast therefore in the liberty wherewith Christ hath made us free, and be not entangled again with the yoke of bondage." More famous, perhaps, is the inscription on the Liberty Bell: "Proclaim liberty throughout all the land unto all the inhabitants thereof" (Lev. 25:10).[100]

Critics of the proposition that America had a Christian founding like to point out that the religious and civic leaders who appealed to verses such as these sometimes took them out of context.[101] These criticisms are not unreasonable, but at a deeper level, it is clear that America's founders understood civic liberty in a thoroughly Christian context. In his inaugural law lecture, a major public event attended by "the President of the United States, with his lady—also the Vice-President, and both houses of Congress, the President and both houses of the Legislature of Pennsylvania, together with a great number of ladies and gentlemen,"[102] James Wilson made what everyone present would have considered to be a commonsensical observation: "Without liberty, law loses its nature and its name, and becomes oppression. Without law, liberty also loses its nature and its name, and becomes licentiousness."[103] The founders distinguished between liberty and licentiousness; they thought the former deserved protection, but not the latter.[104]

In the twentieth century, Supreme Court justices held that the First Amendment protects the right to use profanity in public,[105] burn the American flag as a form of political protest,[106] and publish obscene and pornographic works.[107] America's founders, even those most influenced by the Enlightenment, would have disagreed. At the time, states routinely adopted constitutional provisions and statutes protecting freedom of speech and press *and* laws banning blasphemy, pornography, obscenity, and other types of speech.[108]

An originalist understanding of the First Amendment does not require states or the national government to protect licentiousness. But there are good, prudential reasons for embracing an expansive understanding of freedom of speech today.[109] Poorly written hate-speech laws, or their selective enforcement, have been used in other countries to stifle politically incorrect speech. For instance, in Sweden, a pastor was sentenced to a month in jail for preaching a sermon deemed to be offensive to homosexuals. His conviction was eventually overturned, but similar laws have been adopted, or are being considered, in other "progressive" countries.[110] Fortunately, in America, courts have interpreted the First Amendment to protect a robust view of free speech that permits pastors and other citizens to share views deemed "offensive" by some cultural elites. But we should all keep in mind the founders' distinction between liberty and license: some speech may be legal, but not moral.

NO RELIGIOUS TEST FOR OFFICE

Academics and popular authors who claim that America has a godless constitution relish pointing out that most state constitutions in the era had religious tests for public office, whereas the federal Constitution does not.[111] They are correct. Even tolerant Quaker Pennsylvania stipulated in its 1776 constitution that legislators must subscribe to the following oath:

> I do believe in one God, the creator and governor of the universe, the rewarder of the good and the punisher of the wicked. And I do

acknowledge the Scriptures of the Old and New Testament to be given by Divine inspiration.[112]

The US Constitution departed from the practices of most states by not including a religious test. Indeed, Article VI goes so far as to ban them:

> The Senators and Representatives before mentioned, and the members of the several State Legislatures, and all executive and judicial officers, both of the United States and of the several States, shall be bound by oath or affirmation, to support this Constitution; but *no religious test shall ever be required as a qualification to any office or public trust under the United States.*[113] (emphasis added)

This provision provoked a great deal of controversy during the ratification debates. Critics of the clause claimed, accurately, that "a Papist or Infidel" or "pagans, deists, and Mahometans" might be elected to office.[114] Proponents of the Constitution seldom denied that these outcomes would be problematic; instead, they responded that such tests were either ineffective or unnecessary. For instance, Oliver Ellsworth, a pious Calvinist from Connecticut, observed that "an unprincipled man, who believes neither the Word nor the being of a God," would not hesitate to "dissemble." Test laws, he concluded, "are utterly ineffectual; they are no security at all, because men of loose principles will, by an external compliance, evade them."[115]

Taking a somewhat different tack, North Carolina governor Samuel Johnson contended in the first of his state's two ratification conventions (the first failed to ratify the proposed constitution) that American citizens were overwhelmingly Christian, that the children of non-Christian immigrants would likely become Christians, and that this would "add to the progress of the Christian religion among us."[116] There is little reason to believe, he implied, that Christians would elect non-Christians or atheists to civic offices.

JACOB HENRY

North Carolina governor Samuel Johnson's assumption that Christians would elect only Christians to office was proven incorrect when voters elected a Jewish citizen, Jacob Henry, to North Carolina's legislature in 1808, despite a state constitutional requirement that "no person, who shall deny the being of God or the truth of the Protestant religion, or the divine authority either of the Old or New Testaments, or who shall hold religious principles incompatible with the freedom and safety of the State, shall be capable of holding any office or place of trust or profit in the civil department within this State."[117]

Henry was reelected in 1809, but at the next legislative session, a fellow legislator objected that he was ineligible for office because he was not a Christian. After an impassioned speech by Henry, the legislature permitted him to retain his seat.[118]

North Carolina's religious test for office was amended in 1868 to permit all theists to hold civic office. To this day, the state's constitution does not permit atheists to hold public office (a provision that has been unenforceable since 1961).[119]

America's founders banned religious tests for federal offices for three major reasons. First, like Governor Johnson, many assumed that Americans would only elect Christians to high political office. Second, although America was populated mostly by Christians, there were many different denominations. So developing a test acceptable to all groups would have been problematic. Finally, some founders were coming to recognize that voters may prefer a competent, reasonable candidate of a different faith tradition to an incompetent, unreasonable member of their own tradition.[120]

It is important to understand what Article VI does and does not require. Article VI prohibits Congress from creating a religious test for federal offices. But citizens may vote based on whatever criteria they consider to be important, and religion or irreligion *may* factor into their decisions. To this day, Americans are less likely to vote for an atheist presidential candidate than for members of any other demographic group.[121] The Constitution clearly leaves such choices to the voters.

CONCLUSION

Those who argue that the United States has a godless Constitution must do more than point out that the Deity is not referenced, or is referenced only once, in our nation's fundamental law. Far more relevant are the religious convictions of the framers and ratifiers, and the sources and ideas from which they drew as they created America's constitutional order. As we have seen, there is no good reason to accept the assertion that "many" or "most" of the founders were deists or even heterodox Christians, whereas there are excellent reasons to believe that they were influenced by the Bible and Christian political ideas. The constitutional order they designed, one characterized by federalism, separation of powers, and checks and balances, reflects their Christian commitments. Their understanding of rights and liberty is best comprehended by taking into account their Christian worldview.

The founders drew from their Christian convictions to design a constitutional system that would protect the rights of all Americans—religious or not. Our civic leaders, and especially Supreme Court justices, have turned some of these convictions on their heads. Some things have improved dramatically since the eighteenth century—the abolition of slavery and eradication of Jim Crow legislation being among the most obvious advances. But in other areas, such as the protection of innocent life and the conviction that the national government is one of limited, enumerated powers, our abandonment of the founders' convictions is a cause for great concern. Similarly, much harm has been done by ignoring the founders' views of religious liberty and church-state relations. It is to these issues that we now turn.

SUGGESTIONS FOR
FURTHER READING

Hall, Mark David. *Roger Sherman and the Creation of the American Republic*. New York: Oxford University Press, 2013. Explores the contributions Sherman and other Reformed Protestants made in the founding era.

Lutz, Donald S. "The Relative Influence of European Writers on Late Eighteenth-Century American Political Thought." *American Political Science Review* 78 (1984): 189–97. An important academic study that shows the founders referenced the Bible in their political writings far more than any other text.

Shain, Barry Alan. *The Myth of American Individualism: The Protestant Origins of American Political Thought*. Princeton University Press, 1994. A rigorous academic study of the impact Protestantism had on the political ideas of many of America's founders.

CHAPTER 3

THOMAS JEFFERSON, JAMES MADISON, AND THE FIRST AMENDMENT

Madison . . . became a dogged secular
advocate of church-state separation.
FORREST CHURCH, THE SEPARATION OF CHURCH AND STATE

[Jefferson's] words "a wall of separation between church and state" are
not simply a metaphor of one private citizen's language; they reflect
accurately the intent of those most responsible for the First Amendment.
R. FREEMAN BUTTS, THE AMERICAN TRADITION IN RELIGION AND EDUCATION

James Madison was a strict separationist. (emphasis original)
STEVEN WALDMAN, FOUNDING FAITH

[Madison] was aiming at absolute separation of church and
state and total exclusion of government aid to religion.
IRVING BRANT, JAMES MADISON: FATHER OF THE CONSTITUTION, 1787–1800

Madison, in fact, had an exquisite sense of the separate
jurisdictions of religion and government, and he shared Jefferson's
belief in a high wall of separation between the two.
LEONARD W. LEVY, ORIGINS OF THE BILL OF RIGHTS[1]

The First Amendment to the United States Constitution begins: "Congress shall make no law respecting an establishment of religion." This provision, referred to as the Establishment Clause, has been interpreted by federal courts to prohibit government support for religion. Until 1947, the amendment restricted only the federal government, but in the case of *Everson v. Board of Education*, the Supreme Court decided that it applied to states as well.[2] Jurists and activists have argued that the clause prohibits, among other things, state aid to religious schools,[3] accommodations that protect religious citizens,[4] and the inclusion of the words "under God" in the Pledge of Allegiance.[5]

Both the majority and the dissenting opinions in *Everson* insisted that the Establishment Clause must be interpreted in light of the founders' views. Justice Wiley Rutledge observed that "no provision of the Constitution is more closely tied to or given content by its generating history than the Religious Clause of the First Amendment. It is at once the refined product and the terse summation of that history."[6] Particularly critical for understanding the creation of the Religion Clauses, in his account, are James Madison's "Memorial and Remonstrance Against Religious Assessments" (1785) and Thomas Jefferson's "Bill for Establishing Religious Freedom" (1786), which became "warp and woof of our constitutional tradition."[7]

Justice Hugo Black agreed with Rutledge that the founders' views are controlling. He contended,

[The] Court has previously recognized that the provisions of the First Amendment, in the drafting and adoption of which Madison and Jefferson played such leading roles, had the same objective and were intended to provide the same protection against governmental intrusion on religious liberty as the Virginia statute.[8]

Black concluded his opinion with the observation that the "First Amendment has erected a wall between church and state. That wall must be kept high and impregnable. We could not approve the slightest breach."[9] He was alluding, of course, to Jefferson's famous 1802 letter to the Danbury Baptists where our third president asserted that the First Amendment requires "a wall of separation between Church & State."[10]

In *Everson*, Black and Rutledge presented an argument that has had a tremendous influence on how courts have interpreted the Establishment Clause. I call it "*Everson*'s syllogism," and it goes as follows:

1. The Establishment Clause must be interpreted in light of the founders' views.
2. Thomas Jefferson and James Madison represent the founders.
3. Jefferson and Madison desired the strict separation of church and state.
4. Therefore, the Establishment Clause requires the strict separation of church and state.

This argument is flawed in multiple ways. Most critically, it ignores the contributions that literally hundreds of other founders made to drafting, debating, and ratifying the First Amendment. I provide evidence to support this claim in this and the following chapter, but in this chapter I also undertake a more difficult task. First, I challenge the conventional wisdom, shared by even serious jurists and scholars, that Jefferson and Madison had significant influence on the men who drafted and ratified the First Amendment. Second, I contend that although Jefferson and Madison wanted to separate church and state more thoroughly than most founders, even they did not embrace the sort of strict separation desired today by groups such as the American Civil Liberties Union and Americans United for Separation of Church and State.[11]

PROTESTANTS AND OTHER AMERICANS UNITED FOR SEPARATION OF CHURCH AND STATE

Americans United for Separation of Church and State was originally named Protestants and Other Americans United for Separation of Church and State, which helps highlight the profound anti-Catholic animus that motivated many separationists in the mid-nineteenth to the mid-twentieth centuries. Philip Hamburger, professor of law at Columbia Law School, documents this animus in detail in his marvelous book *Separation of Church and State*.[12] Among other things, he shows that one of the authors of *Everson's* syllogism, Hugo Black, had been a member of the Ku Klux Klan.[13] He also observes that "in the late 1940s, at least seven justices of the Supreme Court belonged to one Masonic organization or the other."[14] The Klan was (and is) more aggressively anti-Catholic than the Masons, but Masons had traditionally been suspicious of Catholic power, and many remained so into the twentieth century.

JEFFERSON'S INFLUENCE HAS
BEEN WILDLY EXAGGERATED

Jefferson was a brilliant man who made important contributions to the creation of the American republic, but this does not mean that he was responsible for everything that happened in the founding era. Jurists, scholars, and academics regularly turn to him to cast light on the First Amendment, often ignoring the reality that he played *no* role in crafting it. In fact, he was not even in the United States when it was drafted by the First Federal Congress; he was ably serving his nation as ambassador to France. Jefferson returned to America while some state legislatures were debating whether to approve the amendment, but there are no records of him participating in any of these debates or attempting to influence them.

None of these inconvenient truths matter, according to strict separationists, because Jefferson drafted the Virginia Statute for Religious Freedom. They contend that this law, penned in 1777 and passed by the state's General Assembly in 1786, inspired and guided the men who created the First Amendment. For instance, the attorney-scholar Leo Pfeffer argued that the Virginia Statute "has long been recognized as the progenitor of the First Amendment's Religious Clauses."[15] Likewise, Martin Marty, one of the most prominent students of America's religious history, contends that "whoever wishes to engage in archeology to understand the text and context of the First Amendment does well to focus on the Virginia Statute."[16] Religion scholar William Lee Miller, in a chapter on the Virginia Statute, averred that Jefferson's "conception of religious liberty, and complete separation of church and state, did come soon to prevail: in the constitutions of other states, in the First Amendment, in the mind of the public."[17] Historian Paul Lucas wrote that the "architects" of the Constitution and Bill of Rights "followed the lead of Thomas Jefferson's famous 'Bill for Establishing Religious Freedom' (adopted by the Virginia House of Delegates in 1786) by separating church and state at the national level."[18] And many additional examples could be given.

National Religious Freedom Day is celebrated every year on January 16, the day the Virginia General Assembly passed the Statute for Religious Freedom. A pamphlet entitled *Religious Freedom Day Guidebook* informs educators that the "men who drafted the US Constitution leaned heavily on Jefferson's Statute in establishing the First Amendment's guarantee of religious freedom."[19] In his 2010 National Religious Freedom Day Proclamation, President Barack Obama asserted that "the First Amendment of our Bill of Rights followed the Virginia Statute's model." Similarly, in 2012, Obama observed that "the Virginia Statute formed the basis for the First Amendment."[20]

The Virginia Statute was approved before the First Amendment, but to assert that for this reason the former influenced the latter is to commit any number of historical fallacies—most clearly that of *post hoc ergo propter hoc* ("after this, therefore because of this").[21] Indeed, between 1776 and 1791, *most* states adopted new constitutional provisions and/or laws concerning religious liberty and church-state relations. Justices, academics, and others who want to argue that the framers of the First Amendment were influenced by the Virginia Statute, or any other text, need to provide *evidence* to support their claim. In this case, the evidence is slight indeed.

It is true that the Virginia Statute was circulated widely after it became law, but this was because, after the assembly passed it, Jefferson "promptly had it printed and he circulated it as widely as he could," in the words of one of Jefferson's best biographers.[22] It was published in at least sixteen American newspapers between 1785 and 1791, but it inspired few responses.[23] Newspaper editors republishing the Virginia Statute occasionally commented on the law, but many of their remarks were vague, such as when the *Pennsylvania Herald* called the act "novel in its kind"[24] or when the Middlesex Connecticut *Gazette* noted that Virginia's General Assembly "passed no less than one hundred and twelve acts: a copy of one of which follows."[25]

The only serious engagement with the Virginia Statute was an attack on it entitled "Considerations on an Act of the Legislature of Virginia, Entitled an Act for the Establishment of Religious Freedom" by John Swanwick, who wrote under the pseudonym "a citizen of Philadelphia." Swanwick's essay was printed in Philadelphia in 1786 by Robert Aitken, who was the first publisher of an English language Bible in America.[26] Addressed to "the Reverend Clergy of all Christian denominations in the City of Philadelphia," Swanwick began by insisting that he supported the toleration of religious minorities.[27] Yet, because Christianity promotes virtue and keeps vice at bay, he argued that "it must unquestionably be the duty of every man to contribute to the support of some religious society or other of those that prevail in the country he lives in, at least as far as the good order shall require, however his private opinion may differ from those of the generality as to the belief thereof."[28] Just as states taxed everyone to support the War of Independence, it is reasonable to require everyone to support a Christian church. The "good order [of society] . . . requires that any small part of it who may differ from the rest, should acquiesce in measures adopted for the general good."[29] Also, "a citizen" thought it prudent to exclude non-Christians from public office, as was then the practice in Pennsylvania and many other states.

The point here is not that Swanwick was correct, but simply that the Virginia Statute was not met with universal approval. It bears emphasizing that the *only* substantial response to the law was negative. Mostly, it was ignored. From the time the Virginia Statute was debated in the Virginia Assembly to the ratification of the First Amendment, the Confederation Congress, several state legislatures, and the new national Congress all passed laws and/or constitutional provisions concerning religion. There are no records of the Virginia Statute being referenced in any of the debates over these measures, nor was language borrowed from it for other statutes.[30] Let's consider a few of the more important debates.

In July 1787, the Confederation Congress passed the Northwest Ordinance, a statute that protected religious liberty in territories controlled by the national government. It proclaimed that "religion, morality, and knowledge being necessary to good government and the happiness of mankind, schools and the means of education shall forever be encouraged."[31] Jefferson would have supported its guarantee of religious freedom, but he might have disagreed with the law's suggestion that governments can encourage religion or religious education.[32] No delegate is recorded as referring to the Virginia Statute or Jefferson, but Nathan Dane, who was intimately involved in drafting the ordinance, later wrote that it "was framed, mainly, from the laws of Massachusetts."[33] He may have had in mind the Massachusetts Constitution of 1780, which maintains that:

> As the happiness of a people, and the good order and preservation of civil government, essentially depend upon piety, religion, and morality . . . the people of this commonwealth have a right to invest their legislature with power to authorize and require . . . the institution of the public worship of GOD, and for the support

and maintenance of public Protestant teachers of piety, religion, and morality, in all cases where such provision shall not be made voluntarily.[34]

The New Hampshire Constitution of 1784, the Vermont Constitution of 1786, and Connecticut's 1784 religious liberty statute, each incorporated language from Article III of the Massachusetts Constitution.[35] Virginia, North Carolina, and Rhode Island borrowed language from Article XVI of Virginia Declaration of Rights (1776) when they proposed religious liberty amendments to the US Constitution.[36] By way of contrast, there is no record of civic officials utilizing the Virginia Statute as a model for a constitutional provision or law prior to the adoption of the First Amendment.[37] Hence, one could reasonably argue that Massachusetts's Article III and Virginia's Article XVI had more influence in the 1780s than did the Virginia Statute for Religious Freedom.

On February 29, 1788, the Confederation Congress voted to pay congressional chaplains $300 per year.[38] Once the Constitution was ratified, the new Congress met and appointed a committee to select chaplains, and within days, Congress had selected and agreed to pay legislative chaplains.[39] The new national government also reauthorized the Northwest Ordinance, issued calls for prayer and fasting, and provided for military chaplains.[40] In no instance is anyone recorded as objecting to these acts because they violated the letter or spirit of the Virginia Statute. The same is true for debates on these sorts of issues at the state level, the Constitutional Convention, the state ratifying conventions, the First Federal Congress, and the state legislatures that ratified the First Amendment.[41]

Legislative debates in this era were poorly recorded, so it is possible that someone appealed to the Virginia Statute as an authority or guide in some of these debates. My point is not that the Virginia Statute had *no* influence, but that there is no evidence that it had anywhere near the sort of influence often attributed to it. Given the fact that Jefferson played no role in drafting or ratifying the First Amendment, and that there is minimal evidence that the Virginia Statute or his other writings on religious liberty or church-state relations influenced the men who were involved in these debates, there is little reason to look to him as a guide for interpreting the First Amendment.[42]

Before leaving the Virginia Statute, let's consider what the law accomplished in Virginia itself. It is commonly asserted that it disestablished the Anglican church,[43] yet an excellent argument can be made that this did not occur until 1787. In 1784, the General Assembly passed an act dictating how the Anglican church in Virginia would be governed. Thomas E. Buckley, one of the best students of disestablishment in Virginia, wrote of the 1784 act: "I think that's about as close to an establishment as one can get."[44] Because it was not repealed until 1787, Buckley persuasively contends that 1787 is the date when the Anglican church was disestablished in Virginia.

Jurists and scholars often speak as if church and state were completely and thoroughly separated after the Virginia Statute was passed, but even as he was drafting this law, Jefferson penned statutes stipulating when Virginia governors may issue calls for prayer and fasting (introduced by Madison but never enacted), and punish disturbers of the Sabbath (introduced by Madison and passed in 1786).[45] More broadly, Virginia remained in the business of mixing church and state even in the immediate aftermath of passing the statute. For instance, when the Virginia ratifying convention met to consider the proposed national constitution in 1788, its first act was to select a "unanimously elected chaplain, to attend, every morning, to read prayers, immediately after the bell shall be rung for calling the Convention."[46]

The Virginia Statute has come to play an important role in how some Americans understand the proper relationship between church and state. Advocates of the strict separation of church and state may wish that it had immediate and tremendous influence, but good history must rely on evidence, not wishful thinking. Simply put, there is little reason to conclude that Jefferson influenced the views of the men who drafted, debated, and ratified the First Amendment.

MADISON'S INFLUENCE HAS BEEN EXAGGERATED

Unlike Jefferson, Madison was a member of the First Federal Congress and a significant advocate for the First Amendment. But, as we shall see, he did not act alone. Before turning to debates over the Religion Clauses, it is necessary to consider his famous "Memorial and Remonstrance Against Religious Assessment" (1785). As with the Virginia Statue, jurists and scholars regularly assert that this eloquent petition influenced the men who drafted and ratified the First Amendment. Indeed, Madison's Memorial played a role in defeating a general assessment bill supported by Patrick Henry, but there is little evidence that it affected other debates over religious liberty and church-state relations in the era.

From the colony's inception, the Church of England was the established church in Virginia. Early laws concerning matters of faith were harsh and intolerant, but during the War of Independence, the establishment became mild. In 1776, the General Assembly passed legislation exempting non-Anglicans from laws requiring church attendance, regulating "modes of worship," and paying ecclesiastical taxes.[47] In the same year, Anglicans were excused temporarily from paying ecclesiastical taxes, a practice that was renewed annually until 1779 when taxes to support the established church were abolished altogether.[48] Patrick Henry was troubled by these developments because he thought that state support of Christianity was essential for a healthy society. Accordingly, in 1784, he helped write and advocated for a "Bill Establishing a Provision for Teachers of the Christian Religion."

Henry's bill would have taxed individuals to support the churches to which they belonged, with the exception of "Quakers and Mennonists" who firmly opposed state involvement in such matters. Citizens could also designate their taxes to support "seminaries of learning," a provision presumably aimed at non–church members. The bill likely would have passed if Henry had not been elevated to the governorship, which, at the time, had little power. On Christmas Eve 1784, the legislature voted to postpone taking action so the bill could be printed and citizens could comment on it.[49]

Concerned that the bill could become law in the fall of 1785, Madison wrote his famous Memorial in summer 1785. In it, he powerfully argued in favor of the "unalienable right" to worship God according to "the conviction and conscience of every man."[50] Although it is sometimes described as a rationalist plea for religious freedom informed by Enlightenment thought, Madison made a number of overtly religious arguments. For instance, in the first article, he affirmed (quoting in part from Virginia's Declaration of Rights) that

we hold it for a fundamental and undeniable truth, "that Religion or the duty which we owe to our Creator and the manner of discharging it, can be directed only by reason and conviction, not by force or violence." The Religion then of every man must be left to the conviction and conscience of every man; and it is the right of every man to exercise it as these may dictate. This right is in its nature an unalienable right. It is unalienable, because the opinions of men, depending only on the evidence contemplated by their own minds cannot follow the dictates of other men: It is unalienable also, because what is here a right towards men, is a duty towards the Creator. It is the duty of every man to render to the Creator such homage and such only as he believes to be acceptable to him. This duty is precedent, both in order of time and in degree of obligation, to the claims of Civil Society.[51]

Later in the document, Madison explicitly reasoned that state subsidies "weaken in those who profess this Religion a pious confidence in its innate excellence and the patronage of its Author" and that "the policy of the Bill is adverse to the diffusion of the light of Christianity."[52]

Thirteen copies of the Memorial signed by 1,552 citizens were submitted to the General Assembly. Altogether, the assembly received about 90 petitions signed by 10,929 Virginians.[53] Far more popular than Madison's Memorial was an earlier evangelical petition signed by 4,899 citizens (including 11 women), which is worth quoting at some length:

Your Petitioners do therefore most earnestly declare against [Henry's bill], believing it to be contrary to the spirit of the Gospel. . . .

Certain it is that the Holy Author of our religion not only supported and maintained his Gospel in the world for several hundred years without the aid of civil power, but against all the powers of the Earth. The excellent purity of its precepts and the unblamable behavior of its ministers (with the divine blessing) made its way through all opposition. Nor was it the better for the Church when Constantine first established Christianity by human laws. . . .

Let ministers manifest to the world "that they are inwardly moved by the Holy Ghost to take upon them that Office," that they seek the good of mankind and not worldly interest. Let their doctrines be Scriptural and their lives upright. Then shall religion (if departed) speedily return, and deism be put to open shame and its dreaded consequences removed.[54]

As suggested by both of these petitions, Americans were turning against religious establishments. But, as we shall see in detail later, they were questioning them because they believed they hurt rather than helped Christianity. Many Americans remained comfortable with other forms of state encouragement of religion.

For present purposes, it is important to emphasize that even in the debate over Patrick Henry's bill, Madison's voice was not the loudest or the most influential; the evangelical petition received far more signatures than Madison's. Yet this reality is ignored regularly by serious scholars who should know better. Law professor and historian Steven K. Green, for instance, wrote that although "Madison's Memorial was not the sole memorial opposing the assessment bill, it was the most influential and helped to turn the tide of public opinion."[55] But he gives no evidence to support this claim. Similarly, historian Daniel M. Calhoon asserts that "Madison's treatise inspired more than ninety anti-assessment petitions, signed by more than eleven thousand citizens."[56] It is difficult to see how this could be the case as the far more popular evangelical petition quoted above was written *at least seven months* before Madison penned his Memorial.

Madison sent copies of his Memorial to George Nicholas and George Mason in summer 1785. He insisted on anonymity and did not explicitly acknowledge writing the text until 1826.[57] The Memorial was published in the *Virginia Journal and Alexandria Advertiser* on November 17, 1785, and the *Massachusetts Spy* on February 2, 1786. Later, in 1786, the Massachusetts publisher Isaiah Thomas reprinted the Memorial together with the Virginia Statute as a pamphlet. It appeared in a few other papers prior to 1790, but was not reprinted again until 1810, when it was published as an appendix to Robert Semple's *History of the Rise and Progress of the Baptists in Virginia*.[58] This is the first time Madison was credited publicly as its author.[59]

The Memorial was signed by 1.6 percent of Virginia's voters, and it must have been considered by other citizens. But not everyone who read Madison's arguments agreed with them. George Mason sent a copy of the Memorial to George Washington, hoping to enlist his support. The future president apparently skimmed the document, promised to read it "with attention" later, and then wrote that "I must confess, that I am not amongst the number of those who are so much alarmed at the thoughts of making people pay towards the support of that which they profess."[60] Washington did not sign a copy of the Memorial submitted to the General Assembly.[61] Other significant civic leaders, including Spencer Roane, Benjamin Harrison, John Page, Edmund Pendleton, Philip Barbour, and future Chief Justice John Marshall supported the general assessment bill.[62]

As with the Virginia Statute, I could find no record of any civic leader being influenced by, or appealing to, Madison's Memorial prior to the ratification of the Bill of Rights.[63] Why, then, do jurists and scholars regularly turn to the document as the key for understanding the First Amendment? From 1947 to 2011, Supreme Court justices cited the Memorial in twenty-four Religion Clause cases, and the petition was reprinted in full as an appendix in two of them.[64]

Separationist jurists and scholars are infatuated with the Memorial, but they are generally uninterested in Madison's argument that Henry's bill "is adverse to the diffusion of the light of Christianity."[65] Instead, they are drawn to his observation that "the same authority which can force a citizen to contribute three pence only of his property to support of any one establishment, may force him to conform to any other establishment in all cases whatsoever."[66] Taken literally, Madison seems to be saying that governments should provide no aid to religious organizations whatsoever. This logic has been used by justices and others who would deny tax-exempt status to churches,[67] prohibit federal funds from purchasing instructional materials for use in religious schools,[68] keep states from offering tax credits to parents who send their children to faith-based schools,[69] and prevent a Lutheran preschool from benefiting from a state program that provides safe playground surfaces.[70]

To challenge the claim that Madison's Memorial influenced the men who drafted and ratified the First Amendment is not to say that he did not play an important role in crafting this amendment. Madison forcefully advocated a bill of rights in the First Federal Congress at a time when many of his colleagues thought one to be unimportant or unnecessary. In a major speech on June 8, 1789, he proposed a host of amendments, but the House declined to discuss them at that time. Madison pushed the issue again on July 21, but was again put off, although this time the House approved a motion by Fisher Ames to form a select committee composed of one member from each state to consider amendments. Madison served on the committee, but it was chaired by John Vining of Delaware. There is no reason to believe that Vining, or seasoned statesmen on the committee such as Roger Sherman, Elias Boudinot, and Abraham Baldwin, simply deferred to their colleague from Virginia. There are no records of the committee's deliberations, but it did produce a draft bill of rights in Sherman's handwriting.[71]

The select committee eventually issued a report proposing nineteen additions to the Constitution. The full House debated these proposed amendments, not the amendments suggested by Madison on June 8, 1789. Madison and a majority of the committee thought the amendments should be interspersed throughout the Constitution, but Sherman objected, arguing that

> we cannot incorporate these amendments in the body of the Constitution. It would be mixing brass, iron, and clay [Dan. 2:35]. . . . I conceive that we have no right to do this, as the Constitution is an act of the people, and ought to remain entire—whereas the amendments will be the act of the several legislatures.

Sherman was overruled, but he eventually won the day and the amendments were annexed to the Constitution rather than interspersed throughout as desired by Madison.[72]

Madison originally offered three amendments that touched on religion: (1) "The civil rights of none shall be abridged on account of religious belief or worship, nor shall any national religion be established, nor shall the full and equal rights of conscience be in any manner, or on any pretext infringed." (2) "No person religiously scrupulous of bearing arms, shall be compelled to render military service in person." (3) "No state shall violate the equal rights of conscience."[73] He considered the third proposal to be "the most valuable amendment" of all, but it was rejected by the Senate, and he was unable to save it.[74] Nor was he successful in passing the second, protecting religious pacifists.

On August 22, 1789, the House appointed Sherman, Egbert Benson, and Theodore Sedgwick—not Madison—to "prepare an introduction to and arrangement of Articles of Amendment."[75] Their report consisted of sixteen articles and was sent to the Senate, which amended and returned them to the House. The House agreed to some of the Senate's amendments, disagreed with others, and appointed Madison, Sherman, and John Vining to a conference committee to reconcile the differences. The Senate chose Oliver Ellsworth to head the Senate delegation. He was joined by Charles Carroll and William Paterson. The committee eventually reported twelve proposed amendments (in Ellsworth's handwriting), which the House approved with a few minor changes. The Senate approved the twelve amendments passed by the House, and they were sent to the states, where the ten that we now know as the Bill of Rights were quickly ratified. Particularly relevant for our purposes is the final wording of the First Amendment's Religion Clauses: "Congress shall make no law respecting an establishment of religion, or prohibiting the free exercise thereof."[76]

Madison deserves credit, perhaps more than any other single individual, for the Bill of Rights and the First Amendment. Yet, as my brief treatment makes clear, he was not a god among men imposing his personal views on cowed colleagues. Approximately eighty-seven representatives and senators participated in the debates and voted for or against what became the First Amendment. And a list of those who played significant roles, besides Madison, must include Roger Sherman, Oliver Ellsworth, Benjamin Huntington, Abraham Baldwin, Elias Boudinot, William Paterson, Samuel Livermore, Charles Carroll, and Fisher Ames.

It is at best simplistic, and at worst dishonest, to ignore the role a host of founders played in drafting, debating, and approving the First Amendment. And yet this is exactly what Supreme Court justices have done. Consider the following comparison: Roger Sherman, like Jefferson, authored a significant state law concerning religious liberty (discussed in the next chapter), but, unlike Jefferson, he participated in congressional debates over the First Amendment and served on key committees. However, when justices have turned to the founders to help them interpret the First Amendment's Religion Clauses, they have made 112 distinct references to Jefferson and 189 references to Madison, but have mentioned Sherman *only 3 times*. Indeed, excluding Madison, justices have made only 21 references to all the other members of the First Congress combined! If jurists or scholars are truly interested in the original intent of those who drafted the First Amendment, it makes little sense to ignore the views and actions of Sherman and most of his colleagues.[77]

JEFFERSON AND MADISON ON CHURCH AND STATE

Jefferson and Madison are two of the most important founders, but this is not a good reason to interpret the First Amendment solely in light of their views. They desired a stricter separation of church and state than most of their colleagues, but the extent to which they desired to separate the two has been exaggerated by jurists and scholars. Moreover, whatever theoretical commitments they may have had, in practice, neither was the sort of strict separationist portrayed by many authors and activists.

Thomas Jefferson

Much of what separationists think they know about Jefferson's views on church-state relations comes from the short missive he sent to the Danbury Baptist Association in 1802. In it, he famously observed that the First Amendment created a "wall of separation between Church & State."[78] This metaphor lay dormant with respect to the Supreme Court's Establishment Clause jurisprudence until 1947, when Justices Black and Rutledge seized upon it as the definitive statement of the founders' views on church-state relations.[79] Since then, liberal justices and academics have turned to this letter time and time again when interpreting the Establishment Clause.

As appealing as the wall metaphor is to contemporary activists, it obscures far more than it illuminates. In his excellent book *Thomas Jefferson and the Wall of Separation Between Church and State*, Daniel L. Dreisbach demonstrates that this letter was a profoundly political document. Moreover, the metaphor it contains did not originate with Jefferson, and he used it only once in his life. Even more remarkably, two days after he penned it, Jefferson attended church services in the US Capitol, where he heard John Leland, the great Baptist minister and an opponent of established churches, preach.[80] According to James Hutson, Jefferson worshipped regularly in the Capitol and, in addition, "made executive-branch buildings—the Treasury and the War Office—available for church services."[81]

As governor of Virginia, Jefferson issued a proclamation that encouraged "the good people of this commonwealth" to set apart a day for "public and solemn thanksgiving and prayer to Almighty God," and urged "ministers of religion to meet their respective societies . . . to assist them in their prayers, [to] edify them with their discourses, and generally to perform the sacred duties of their function, proper for the occasion."[82] When he revised Virginia's laws, in addition to crafting his now famous Statute for Religious Freedom, he also drafted bills stipulating when the governor could appoint "days of public fasting and humiliation, or thanksgiving" and to punish "Disturbers of Religious Worship and Sabbath Breakers."[83]

In 1776, the Continental Congress appointed Benjamin Franklin, John Adams, and Jefferson to a committee to begin the process of creating a national seal. Jefferson proposed that the nation adopt one with the images of

> Pharaoh sitting in an open chariot, a crown on his head & a sword in his hand, passing through the divided waters of the Red Sea in pursuit of the Israelites: rays from a pillar of fire in the cloud, expressive of the divine presence & command, reaching to Moses who stands on the shore &, extending his hand over the sea, causes it to overwhelm Pharaoh.[84]

His motto for the new nation would have been: "Rebellion to tyrants is obedience to God."[85] Franklin's proposal was virtually identical to Jefferson's. Only Adams avoided biblical references, preferring instead to draw images from ancient Greece.

Two committees and six years later, Charles Thompson, secretary to Congress and the first American translator of the Bible from Greek to English, finalized America's national seal.[86] Advocates for separating church and state sometimes point out that the words above the pyramid, "annuit coeptis"—often translated as "He favors (or has favored) our undertaking"—do not clearly and indisputably refer to the Christian God.[87] Whatever the merits of this argument, and I think they are few, it is noteworthy that if Jefferson had his way, there would be no doubt that the national seal and motto invoked the God of Abraham, Isaac, and Jacob.[88]

Unlike Washington and Adams, Jefferson refused to issue calls for prayer when he was president of the United States. In an 1808 letter to Samuel Miller, he indicated that both the First and the Tenth Amendments prevented him from doing so. Such calls for prayer, he suggested, should be issued by state governments, if they are to be issued at all.[89] Yet, in more than one speech, he invited his audiences to pray. For instance, Jefferson closed his second inaugural address by noting that he would need "the favor of that Being in whose hands we are, who

Jefferson's proposed national seal was drawn by Benjamin J. Lossing and originally published in the July 1856 issue of *Harpers' New Monthly Magazine*. Courtesy of the American Antiquarian Society.

led our forefathers, as Israel of old," and asked his listeners to "join with me in supplications, that he [God] will so enlighten the minds of your servants, guide their councils, and prosper their measures, that whatsoever they do, shall result in your good, and shall secure to you the peace, friendship, and approbation of all nations."[90]

Most remarkably for someone supposedly committed to a "wall of separation between church and state," Jefferson, in 1803, sent a treaty concerning the Kaskaskia Indians to the Senate for approval. The third article in the treaty stipulated that

> *whereas* the greater part of the said tribe have been baptized and received into the Catholic church, to which they are much attached, the United States will give, annually, for seven years, one hundred dollars towards the support of a priest of that religion, who will engage to perform for the said tribe the duties of his office, and also to instruct as many of their children as possible, in the rudiments of literature. And the United States will further give the sum of three hundred dollars, to assist the said tribe in the erection of a church.[91]

Federal funds to support a Catholic priest and to build a church! So much for a high and impregnable wall of separation between church and state.

The point of this section is *not* that Jefferson was a pious man who wanted a union between church and state. His private letters make it clear that he was not an orthodox Christian, and his public arguments and actions demonstrate that he favored a stricter separation between church and state than virtually any other founder. Yet, even Jefferson, at least in his actions, did not attempt to completely remove religion from the public square—and what Jefferson did not completely exclude, most founders embraced.

James Madison

In 1833, Jasper Adams, a minister and president of the College of Charleston, preached a sermon entitled "The Relation of Christianity to Civil Government in the United States."[92] In it, he expounded on the many ways Christianity supports republican government. Adams sent a published version of the sermon to a plethora of American leaders and asked for their thoughts. Among those who responded were Chief Justice John Marshall, who seconded his view that in America, "it would be strange, indeed, if with such a people, our institutions did not presuppose Christianity."[93] Justice Joseph Story likewise agreed that "Christianity is indispensable to the true interests and solid foundations of all free governments."[94]

James Madison, at age eighty-two, responded as well. In his letter to Adams, he suggested a metaphor different from Jefferson's wall to explain church-state relations in the United States:

> I must admit, moreover, that it may not be easy, in every possible case, to trace the *line of separation*, between the rights of Religion & the Civil authority, with such distinctness, as to avoid collisions & doubts on unessential points.[95] (emphasis added)

Not surprisingly, separationists prefer Jefferson's wall to Madison's line. Perhaps this is because Madison admitted that it is difficult to separate church and state in some cases. And when it is possible to do so, a line is a far less imposing barrier than a wall. This is not to say that Madison, any more than Jefferson, wanted a union between church and state. But throughout his long and illustrious career in public service, he rarely acted as if government should have nothing to do with religion.

For instance, on February 29, 1788, the Confederation Congress voted to pay congressional chaplains $300 per year. Madison was present and voted in favor of doing so.[96] At the Virginia ratifying convention, the delegates voted to appoint and, later, pay a chaplain. Madison, a member of the convention, missed the first vote, and no record was taken of who voted for and against compensating the chaplain.[97] Once the Constitution was ratified, the new Congress met and appointed a committee (on which Madison served) to select chaplains. It did not take Congress long to choose and agree to pay two chaplains, one for each house.[98] The new national government also reauthorized the Northwest Ordinance, requested that the president issue a Thanksgiving Day proclamation, and provided for military chaplains.[99] There is no record of Madison objecting to any of these actions at the time.

Like Jefferson, Madison attended worship services in the US Capitol.[100] He shared his predecessor's distaste for presidential calls for public prayer, but he issued four of them anyway. The second recommends

> to all who shall be piously disposed to unite their hearts and voices in addressing at one and the same time their vows and adorations to the Great Parent and Sovereign of the Universe . . . [supplicating Him to] pardon our manifold transgressions and awaken and strengthen in all the wholesome purposes of repentance and amendment . . . [so that] we may be enabled to beat our swords into plowshares [Isa. 2:4] and to enjoy in peace every man the fruits of his honest industry and rewards of his lawful enterprise.[101]

This proclamation was issued in July 1813, when America's war with Great Britain was at a low point. Madison must have felt immense pressure to issue it, and he went out of his way to emphasize that he was merely *recommending* prayer. Nevertheless, he chose to issue these proclamations, and no one forced him to incorporate Scripture into the one quoted above.

In 1811, Madison vetoed an act that would have incorporated an Episcopal church in the District of Columbia, because he believed it to exceed

> the rightful authority, to which Governments are limited by the essential distinction between Civil and Religious functions, and violates, in particular, the Article of the Constitution of the United States which declares, that "Congress shall make no law respecting a Religious establishment."[102]

Some have accused this church of seeking preferential treatment, but because there was no national general incorporation law, the only way it could incorporate was through special legislation. Nevertheless, Madison's veto provides evidence that he desired a stricter separation of church and state than most of his colleagues.[103]

Even more to the delight of separationists, sometime after his presidency, Madison penned a document known today as the "Detached Memoranda." In this text, which was unpublished in Madison's lifetime and essentially unknown until it was printed in the *William and Mary Quarterly* in 1946, Madison stated that the federal government should not pay chaplains and that presidents should not issue religious proclamations.[104] These post-presidential reflections carry no legal weight, and there is little reason to believe that they reflect Madison's long-held views. It is possible, of course, that he had always held these views even as his actions suggested otherwise. More likely, it seems to me, is that Madison simply changed his mind on these points.

It is sometimes assumed that Madison opposed Patrick Henry's general assessment bill because he was against religion. Late in life, Madison wrote several letters reflecting on the consequences of disestablishing the Anglican church in Virginia. He observed that there is no question that "there has been an increase of religious instruction since the revolution, and that the number, the industry, and the morality of the priesthood and the devotion of the people have been manifestly increased by the total separation of church and state."[105] In 1833, three years before his death, he reiterated these sentiments to Jasper Adams, noting that disestablishment resulted in "the greater purity & industry of the pastors & in the greater devotion of their flocks."[106] In the context of his missives, it is evident that he believed these outcomes were desirable.

Madison thought that establishments hurt rather than helped true religion. But his actions demonstrate that even he did not desire to build a high and impregnable wall of separation between church and state.

CONCLUSION

Jefferson and Madison wanted a greater degree of separation between church and state than most of their colleagues. But even they did not embrace the sort of strict separation advocated today by groups such as the ACLU and Americans United for Separation of Church and State. Even if they did, there is simply no valid reason for reading the First Amendment as if it were solely a product of their two minds. And it certainly shouldn't be viewed through the lens of Jefferson's letter to the Danbury Baptists and Madison's "Detached Memoranda," both of which were penned years after the amendment was ratified. Moreover, when one turns to other founders, including men intimately involved in drafting and ratifying the First Amendment, it becomes evident that Jefferson and Madison do not represent the founding generation's approach to church-state relations.

SUGGESTIONS FOR FURTHER READING

Buckley, Thomas. *Church and State in Revolutionary Virginia.* Charlottesville: University of Virginia Press, 1977. The best history of the debates over disestablishment in Virginia.

Dreisbach, Daniel L. *Thomas Jefferson and the Wall of Separation Between Church and State.* New York: NYU Press, 2002. The definitive account of Jefferson's famous letter to the Danbury Baptists.

Hall, Mark David. "Jeffersonian Walls and Madisonian Lines: The Supreme Court's Use of History in Religion Clause Cases." *High Court Quarterly Review* 5 (2009): 109–53, http://digitalcommons.georgefox.edu/hist_fac/4/. This essay provides an exhaustive overview of how Supreme Court justices have used history to cast light on the First Amendment's Religion Clauses.

Hamburger, Philip. *Separation of Church and State.* Cambridge: Harvard University Press, 2002. An excellent history of the idea that church and state should be separated in America.

The Founders Believed Civic Authorities Should Protect, Promote, and Encourage Religion and Morality

At the national level, [the founders] designed a secular Constitution,
which they reinforced like prudential engineers with the
redundancy of the First Amendment's religious protections.
JONATHAN D. SASSI, "AMERICAN RELIGIOUS ECLECTIC AND SECULAR"

The First Amendment banned government activity in religion generally.
JON BUTLER, "WHY REVOLUTIONARY AMERICA WASN'T A 'CHRISTIAN NATION'"

The dominant view among the founders regarding the religion clauses of the
First Amendment is captured by Jefferson's [wall of separation] metaphor.
JAMES F. HARRIS, THE SERPENTINE WALL

The framers of the Bill of Rights hoped that the First Amendment
would encourage other states to follow Virginia's example and establish
the complete separation between religious and civil authorities.
SUSAN JACOBY, FREETHINKERS

The founders most certainly were secularists who believed in keeping
religion out of politics, and that is enough to place them firmly on
the side of those who object, for example, to ostentatious displays of
the Ten Commandments in government-owned public places.
RICHARD DAWKINS, THE GOD DELUSION[1]

W hen one turns from Jefferson and Madison to the rest of America's civic leaders in the late eighteenth century, it becomes evident that most believed governments should protect, promote, and encourage religion and morality. Many founders had come to question religious establishments because they concluded that they hurt rather than helped Christianity. So instead, they created civic space in which religion could flourish. But that doesn't mean they thought governments shouldn't promote religion at all. And, as noted earlier, by "religion" the vast majority of them meant Christianity.[2] If we take an originalist approach to the First Amendment, it is constitutionally permissible for governments to continue to encourage religion today. Of course, what is permissible may not be prudential. But that is a different discussion. First, let's understand what the founders really thought about government support for religion. I'll begin by discussing how state leaders approached this issue before shifting to the national government.

STATE GOVERNMENTS ON CHURCH AND STATE

Some states never had an established church, and in the 1780s, those that did, either disestablished them or moved to a system of plural or multiple establishments.[3] But most continued to protect, encourage, and support Christianity and/or Christian practices. For example, when delegates met in Philadelphia to draft a new constitution, Georgia, New Hampshire, Massachusetts, New Jersey, North Carolina, South Carolina, Vermont, and even Rhode Island required civic officials to be Protestants, whereas Delaware, Maryland, and Pennsylvania insisted that they must "merely" be Christians. New York and Virginia did not have religious tests, and the interesting case of Connecticut is discussed later in this chapter.[4]

RELIGIOUS TESTS FOR OFFICE

Lists of states that had religious tests vary based on date (e.g., 1776 versus 1787 versus 1800), and sometimes list makers err by considering only constitutional as opposed to statutory tests. New York is an interesting case; it is sometimes labeled as having no religious test and sometimes as permitting only Protestants to hold office. Its 1777 constitution contains no test, but in 1788, the General Assembly passed a law requiring officeholders to "renounce and abjure all allegiance and subjection to all and every foreign king, prince, potentate and State, in all matters ecclesiastical as well as civil."[5] The reference to ecclesiastical authorities was widely understood to prohibit Roman Catholics from holding office. Although it was probably not the legislature's intent, this oath requirement would not have prevented Jewish citizens from holding civic offices.

Of course, some states promoted religion and morality more than others; a good rule of thumb is that the northern states (with the partial exception of Rhode Island) were more engaged in such practices than the southern ones.[6] A full survey of how every state promoted faith goes well beyond the scope of this book, but a brief consideration of three different states (one from each region) and a few lesser-known but still important founders helps show that there is little evidence that America's civic leaders wanted to build a wall of separation between church and state.[7] Indeed, most of them seemed to believe, as evidenced by their words and deeds, that civic authorities should protect, promote, and encourage religion and morality.

Critics of this section may be tempted to dismiss the actions of state legislators as being those of naïve localists. But before doing so, they should remember that most of America's more cosmopolitan founders also served in state governments, and many less famous but still influential founders did as well. Moreover, it was the state legislatures that ratified the First Amendment, and many originalists insist that the amendment should be interpreted in how it was originally *understood*, not by the original *intent* of its drafters. If one takes this approach, there is all the more reason to broaden our conception of who counts as a "founder" beyond the six or seven most famous ones. And sometimes the less famous ones had a lot more influence than we might assume.

Connecticut

Consider, for instance, the case of Connecticut's Roger Sherman. No one considers him to be a famous founder, but he is the only statesman to help draft and sign the Declaration and Resolves (1774), the Articles of Association (1774), the Declaration of Independence (1776), the Articles of Confederation (1777, 1778), and the US Constitution (1787).[8] He served longer in the Continental and Confederation Congresses than all but four men, and he was regularly appointed to key committees, including those charged with drafting the Declaration of Independence and the Articles of Confederation. At the Constitutional Convention, Sherman often outmaneuvered Madison, and, according to David Brian Robertson, the "political synergy between Madison and Sherman . . . may have been necessary for the Constitution's adoption."[9] He was also a representative and senator in the new republic where, among other things, he played a major role in drafting the Bill of Rights.

After America declared independence, many states revised their laws. Connecticut asked Roger Sherman and Richard Law to do so in 1783. They worked on the project throughout the summer and fall, and the General Assembly reviewed their work—accepted, rejected, and amended their proposals—and approved the new state code in January 1784.[10] The alterations as a whole are interesting, and some changes are even inspiring, such as Sherman and Law's proposal that put slavery in the state on the path to extinction, which was adopted by the General Assembly.[11] But particularly relevant for our purposes is the statute Sherman drafted to protect religious liberty in Connecticut. Although it was passed about the time the Virginia Statute became law, and even though Sherman helped draft the First Amendment while Jefferson did not, this Connecticut statute has been almost completely neglected by Supreme Court justices and scholars alike. This is a mistake.

Sherman's religious liberty bill began with a preamble that highlights the importance of religion and the duty of civic authorities to promote the Christian faith:

As the happiness of a people, and the good order of civil society, essentially depend upon piety, religion, and morality, it is the duty of the civil authority to provide for the support and encouragement thereof; so as that Christians of every denomination, demeaning themselves peaceably, and as good subjects of the State, may be equally under the protection of the laws: and as the people of this State have in general, been of one profession in matters of faith, religious worship, and the mode of settling and supporting the ministers of the Gospel, they have by law been formed into Ecclesiastical Societies, for the more convenient support of their worship and ministry: and to the end that other denominations of Christians who differ from the worship and ministry so established and supported, may enjoy free liberty of conscience in the matters aforesaid.[12]

This preamble illustrates well the common view among America's founders that Christianity was necessary for public happiness and political prosperity. Because religion is so important, many founders, especially in New England, continued to believe that governments should support it. This is crystal clear from Connecticut's revised statutes, which among other things:

1. required all citizens "on the Lord's-Day carefully to apply themselves to duties of Religion and Piety, publicly and privately";
2. required all citizens to attend church each Sunday;
3. provided tax money to support churches and ministers;
4. punished Sabbath breakers;
5. required each family to possess a Bible and instructed town leaders to "supply" Bibles and "a suitable Number of Orthodox

Catechisms, and other good Books of practical Godliness" to families in need;

6. required civic officeholders and voters to take oaths witnessed "by the Everlasting GOD";

7. required families who adopted "an Indian Child" to instruct him or her in "the principles of the Christian Religion"; and

8. passed numerous statutes reflecting Christian morality on issues such as adultery, divorce, drunkenness, fornication, gaming, and horse racing.

Some of these provisions were rarely enforced, but it should, nevertheless, be clear that in 1784, Connecticut's civic officials still thought it proper for the state to promote Christianity.[13]

Connecticut's leaders believed that state support for Christianity was compatible with "free liberty of conscience," at least for "Christians of every denomination." And note that rather than favor Congregationalism, as had historically been the practice, the new statutes provided for a plural establishment, whereby individuals would be taxed to support the churches they chose to attend (so long as they chose to attend Protestant churches).[14] These provisions unfairly favored some believers over others, and it is only a partial defense of them that there "were only a handful of Catholics in late eighteenth-century Connecticut and a half-dozen Jews."[15] In other words, 99.99 percent of the state's citizens identified themselves as Protestants. This reality perhaps explains why Connecticut, unlike virtually every other state, didn't have a traditional religious test other than to require freemen and officeholders to take an oath in the name of the "Everliving God."[16] A separate statute permitted Quakers to "affirm" rather than "swear" these oaths.[17]

The other New England states (with the partial exception of Rhode Island) had statutes similar to Connecticut's, and in general remained more convinced that states, rather than the nation, should encourage faith. This is evidenced in part by the survival of plural establishments in these states, until 1807 (Vermont), 1818 (Connecticut), 1819 (New Hampshire), 1820 (Maine), and 1833 (Massachusetts). I have focused on Connecticut because Sherman, and his protégé Oliver Ellsworth, went on to play major roles in drafting the First Amendment.[18] Some twenty-first-century Americans may not like these laws or views, but if we are truly interested in the founders' approach to religious liberty and church-state relations, they cannot be ignored.

Pennsylvania

Pennsylvania was founded by the Quaker William Penn in 1681 as a haven for Quakers and other religious dissenters. Civic officials tolerated non-Quakers, but even they adopted religious tests for office and used the power of the state to promote Christian morality.[19] Quakers lost power in the 1750s, but Pennsylvania continued to protect religious liberty as evidenced by its 1776 constitution, which recognized that "all men have a natural and unalienable right to worship Almighty God according to the dictates of their own conscience."[20] And yet, as was the case in many states, the right to religious liberty went hand in hand with a religious test for political office. In this case, a would-be officeholder had to swear or affirm that:

I do believe in one God, the creator and governor of the universe, the rewarder of the good and the punisher of the wicked. And I do acknowledge the Scriptures of the Old and New Testament to be given by Divine inspiration.[21]

As a practical matter, this test excluded very few citizens from public office, but it did exclude some, notably members of Philadelphia's Jewish community. The constitution also required that: "Laws for the encouragement of virtue, and prevention of vice and immorality, shall be made and constantly kept in force, and provision shall be made for their due execution."[22]

The Pennsylvania Constitution of 1776 stipulated that a "Council of Censors" meet every seven years to determine if the constitution needed to be amended. When this body met in 1783, leaders of Philadelphia's Jewish synagogue submitted a petition requesting that the religious test be revised so that Jews, along with Christians, could hold public office.[23] The petition did not condemn religious tests per se, and it even seems to support banning atheists from public office. The council considered the petition, tabled it, and took no further action. However, when the state rewrote its constitution in 1789–1790, it amended its religious test to permit any "person, who acknowledges the being of a God and a future state of rewards and punishments" to hold public office.[24] This change permitted Jewish citizens to serve as elected officials, but it is not accurate to say that the state "dropped its religious test in 1790" as Isaac Kramnick and R. Laurence Moore assert.[25]

In 1779, Pennsylvania passed an "act for the suppression of vice and immorality." Its preamble gives an excellent sense of what the legislature desired to encourage and discourage:

Whereas sufficient provision has not hitherto been made by law for the due observation of the Lord's day, commonly called Sunday, and the preventing of profane swearing, cursing, drunkenness, cock fighting, bull-baiting, horse racing, shooting matches, and the playing or gaming for money or other valuable things, fighting of duels, and such evil practices, which tend greatly to debauch the minds and corrupt the morals of the subjects of this commonwealth . . .[26]

This five-page law contains too many details to recount here, but it is worth noting that those who participate in staging any "tragedy, comedy or tragi comedy, farce, interlude or other play . . . [shall] forfeit and pay the sum of five hundred pounds."[27]

It is sometimes said that you can't legislate morality, but it is more accurate to say you can't *not* legislate morality. To be sure, laws banning plays are simply imprudent. But even today, we prohibit cockfighting, dueling, and other "evil practices." One of the greatest evils in the founding era was slavery, and in 1780, the Pennsylvania legislators put this vile institution on the road to extinction in their commonwealth. And they did so for theological reasons, explaining that when they reflected on God's deliverance from Great Britain,

we are unavoidably led to a serious and grateful sense of the manifold blessings which we have undeservedly received from the hand of that Being from whom every good and perfect gift cometh [James 1:17]. Impressed with these ideas, we conceive that it is our duty, and we rejoice that it is in our power to extend a portion of that freedom to others, which hath been extended to us; and a release from that state of thralldom to which we ourselves were tyrannically doomed, and from which we have now every prospect of being delivered. It is not for us to enquire why, in the creation of mankind, the inhabitants of the several parts of the earth were distinguished by a difference in feature or complexion. It is sufficient to know that all are the work of an Almighty Hand.[28]

97

One does not need to be a Christian to oppose slavery, but in America, virtually all early abolitionists were motivated by their Christian convictions. We can criticize the General Assembly for not abolishing slavery immediately, but politics is the art of the possible, and a gradual emancipation act is better than no emancipation act at all.

Georgia

The Church of England had been established in Georgia, South Carolina, North Carolina, Virginia, Maryland, and partially established in New York.[29] It is not surprising that during or shortly after the War of Independence—a war fought against *England*—this church was disestablished in each of these states. South Carolina creatively established in its place the "Protestant Christian religion" as the state's official faith in 1778, but this experiment only lasted until 1790.[30] Church and state were more thoroughly separated in the South than in New England, but even in the South there was hardly a wall of separation between the two. Consider, for example, the case of Georgia.

I focus on Georgia because one of the chief architects of church-state relations in the state, Abraham Baldwin, went on to play a significant role in drafting the First Amendment.[31] Baldwin was born in Connecticut, graduated from Yale College, was a tutor at Yale for three years, and served as a full-time chaplain in the Revolutionary army from 1779 to 1783. Yale president Ezra Stiles recruited him to be a professor of divinity, but Baldwin declined and studied law instead. He was licensed as an attorney in 1783, and moved to Georgia in 1784.[32]

Baldwin was elected to Georgia's General Assembly the same year he arrived in the state. After Governor Lyman Hall requested that the legislature design a school system where "every encouragement [is] given to introduce religion,"[33] Baldwin drafted a statute to create a state university and to provide oversight for other public schools in the state. The statute began with a preamble proclaiming that it should be

> among the first objects of those who wish well to the national prosperity, to encourage and support the principles of religion and morality, and early to place the youth under the forming hand of society, that by instruction they may be molded to the love of virtue and good order.[34]

The statute also required that "all officers appointed to the instruction and government of the university shall be of the Christian religion."[35] But, as was the case in many states in this era, this discriminatory law went hand in hand with a religious liberty provision; in this instance, one demanding that

> trustees shall not exclude any person of any religious denomination whatever, from free and equal liberty and advantages of education, or from any of the liberties, privileges, and immunities of the university in his education, on account of his or their speculative sentiments in religion, or being of a different religious profession.[36]

Baldwin's statute favored Christianity with respect to employment, although the provision quoted above prohibits trustees from discriminating against people of a "different religious profession." This part of the law may have been crafted specifically to protect members of Savannah's Jewish community. The legislature approved the bill, and Baldwin was appointed the first president of the University of Georgia (even as he continued to hold other public offices).

In 1785, Baldwin drafted a statute with the title "For the Regular Establishment and Support of the Public Duties of Religion." It began with a preamble declaring that:

> As the knowledge and practice of the principles of the Christian religion tends greatly to make good members of society, as well as good men, and is no less necessary to present, than to future happiness, its regular establishment and support is among the most important objects of legislature determination; and that the minds of the citizens of this state may be properly informed and impressed by the great principles of moral obligation and thus be induced by inclination furnished with opportunity, and favored by law to render public religious honors to the Supreme Being.[37]

The bill guaranteed that "all the different sects and denominations of the Christian religion shall have free and equal liberty and toleration in the exercise of their religion within the state."[38] It also required each county "which contains thirty heads of families" to choose a "Minister of the Gospel who shall on every Sunday publicly explain and inculcate the great doctrines and precepts of the Christian religion."[39] This minister would be supported by public tax revenues, and counties with larger populations could have multiple ministers.

The bill drafted by Baldwin was passed by the state legislature, but apparently its provisions were never acted upon.[40] As in other states, Georgians were coming to question the wisdom of even multiple establishments. Yet this is not to say they embraced the separation of church and state. For instance, in 1786, the state passed a copyright act that specifically denied protection to works "that may be profane, treasonable, defamatory, or injurious to government, morals, or religion."[41]

In addition to serving in Georgia's legislature, Baldwin was a member of the Confederation Congress and a delegate to the Constitutional Convention. In 1788, he was elected to the US House of Representatives, where he served until he was elevated to the Senate in 1800. He was a senator until his death in 1807. With respect to the Bill of Rights, he was a member of the important committee that drafted the amendments debated by the House of Representatives, and he eventually voted to approve the amendments sent to the states for ratification. If jurists and scholars are truly interested in the original meaning of the Establishment Clause, there is no good reason to ignore the views of men like Abraham Baldwin.

Compared to America's earliest colonial settlements, or even to colonial statutes in effect in, say, 1770, states in the early republic were moving away from regulating and funding religion (and especially from favoring a single denomination).[42] Shortly after the ratification of the US Constitution, Georgia, South Carolina, Delaware, Vermont, Tennessee, and Kentucky either removed their religious tests for office or declined to create one.[43] Yet many American founders remained comfortable with the idea that it was appropriate for states to advance religion, especially if they did so in a way that did not discriminate among Christian denominations. Few embraced even a theoretical commitment to strictly separating church and state, but, as we saw with Jefferson and Madison, their practices often fell short of their own supposed ideals. Many of these state leaders went on to play important roles in drafting and ratifying the First Amendment.

CHURCH AND STATE IN THE CONTINENTAL AND CONFEDERATION CONGRESSES

Unlike the states, the Continental and Confederation Congresses had little power to pass legislation that directly restricted or affected individuals. Yet, within their limited sphere of authority, national leaders encouraged religious practices in a variety of ways.

The First Continental Congress convened on September 5, 1774. The next day, Massachusetts's Thomas Cushing proposed that they open their meetings with prayer. Several delegates objected, worried that the body was "so divided in religious sentiments" that they would be unable to agree on a minister to officiate.[44] The Congregationalist Samuel Adams responded that "he was no bigot, and could hear a prayer from a gentleman of piety and virtue." He suggested they invite the Anglican minister Jacob Duché to open the body with prayer.[45] Congress agreed. The following day, Reverend Duché "arrived in his Pontificallibus, read several Prayers," and then, according to John Adams, "struck out into an extemporary prayer, which filled the bosom of every man present."[46]

Duché was formally appointed chaplain to Congress in 1776, but the following year, he was captured by the British and became a loyalist. He fled to England and was unable to return to America until 1792. In December 1776, Congress appointed two chaplains to replace him: an Anglican and a Presbyterian. The Continental and, later, Confederation Congresses continued to utilize two chaplains from different denominations until it disbanded, at which time the First Federal Congress adopted the practice—one that continues to the present day.[47]

Congress was always strapped for cash, but nevertheless, it

agreed in 1775 to create a chaplain corps for the Continental army and pay the ministers who served in it. When Congress later considered the cost-saving measure of having chaplains at the brigade level, rather than the regiment level, General Washington objected.[48] Throughout the war, Washington encouraged his officers and men to attend worship services. At Valley Forge, for instance, he issued the following order:

> The Commander-in-Chief directs that divine service be performed every Sunday at 11 o'clock in each brigade which has a chaplain. Those brigades which have none will attend the places of worship nearest to them. It is expected that officers of all ranks will, by their attendance, set an example to their men. While we are duly performing the duty of good soldiers, we certainly ought not to be inattentive to the higher duties of religion. To the distinguished character of a Patriot, it should be our highest glory to add the more distinguished character of a Christian.
>
> The signal instances of Providential goodness which we have experienced, and which have almost crowned our arms with complete success, demand from us, in a peculiar manner, the warmest returns of gratitude and piety to the Supreme Author of all good.[49]

Washington "expected" but did not order his officers to attend divine services, and enlisted men were apparently free to worship or not as their consciences dictated. Some states required members of their militia to attend such services. Connecticut, for instance, stipulated that "all officers and soldiers, not having just impediment, shall diligently frequent divine service and sermon in the places appointed for assembling the regiment, troop or company."[50] Congress could have similarly demanded that soldiers in the Continental army participate in church services, but instead it passed military regulations that "earnestly *recommended* to all officers and soldiers, diligently to attend Divine Service"[51] (emphasis added).

The Continental and Confederation Congresses issued more than a dozen calls for prayer, fasting, and thanksgiving. The first one encouraged "Christians, of all denominations, to assemble for public worship" on July 20, 1775.[52] On that day, "Congress attended *en masse* Reverend Duché's Episcopal church in the morning, and Dr. Francis Allison's First Presbyterian Church in the afternoon."[53] Two years later, Congress observed that it is the "indispensable duty of all men to adore the superintending providence of Almighty God," and encouraged citizens to "join the penitent confession of their manifold sins, whereby they had forfeited every favor, and their humble and earnest supplication that it may please God, through the merits of Jesus Christ, mercifully to forgive and blot them out of remembrance." The call ends by recommending that Americans ask God "to prosper the means of religion for the promotion and enlargement of that kingdom which consisteth in 'righteousness, peace and joy in the Holy Ghost' [Rom. 14:17]."[54]

In like fashion, in May 1778, Congress "recommended to ministers of the gospel of all denominations to read or cause to be read, immediately after divine services," an address by Congress "in their respective churches and chapels, and other places of divine worship."[55] As with earlier calls, this address proclaimed that America is relying on God's providential care, incorporated Scripture into the text without citation (e.g., "the time will soon arrive when every man shall sit under his own vine and under his own fig-tree, and there shall be none to make him afraid [Mic. 4:4]"), and encouraged Americans to "assiduously cultivate . . . [the] assistance of Heaven."[56]

In 1781, Congress turned to one of America's finest theologians to draft calls for prayer: John Witherspoon, a Presbyterian minister who was serving simultaneously as president of the College of New Jersey (now Princeton) and as a delegate to Congress from New Jersey.[57] Witherspoon drafted a request that states set apart December 13, 1781,

> to be religiously observed as a Day of Thanksgiving and Prayer; that all the people may assemble on that day, with grateful hearts, to celebrate the praises of our gracious Benefactor; to confess our manifold sins; to offer up our most fervent supplications to the God of all grace, that it may please Him to pardon our offences, and incline our hearts for the future to keep all his laws . . . and cause the knowledge of God to cover the earth, as the waters cover the seas.[58]

Congress regularly encouraged, but had no power to require, civic and religious leaders to set aside time to pray. Some of these calls referred to God with phrases like "Supreme Ruler," "Almighty Being," and "great Creator,"[59] yet if one considers the individuals who wrote, approved, and read these calls, there is little question that they understood them to refer to the God of Christianity—a Deity that most certainly intervenes in the affairs of men and nations.

Congress encouraged citizens to be virtuous, and it sometimes asked state leaders to adopt laws promoting morality.[60] For instance, in 1778, it approved a resolution stating:

Whereas true religion and good morals are the only solid foundations of public liberty and happiness:

Resolved, that it be, and it is hereby earnestly recommended to the several States, to take the most effectual measures for the encouragement thereof, and for the suppressing of theatrical entertainments, horse racing, gaming, and such other diversions as are productive of idleness, dissipation, and a general depravity of principles and manners.

Resolved, that all officers in the army of the United States, be, and hereby are strictly enjoined to see that the good and wholesome rules provided for the discountenancing of prophaness and vice, and the preservation of morals among the soldiers, are duly and punctually observed.[61]

Congress overwhelmingly approved these resolutions, but they were not always unanimous. Some representatives from southern states were, it seems, less than thrilled about condemning horse racing.[62]

Before the War of Independence, Americans imported Bibles from Great Britain. The war curtailed this trade, leading to a shortage of this sacred text. In 1777, a group of ministers asked Congress to address this problem. Congress initially approved the importation of twenty thousand Bibles at its own expense, but this motion was ultimately tabled—almost certainly because it lacked funds. Four years later, Robert Aitken, a Presbyterian elder and congressional printer, asked Congress to authorize him to publish the first American edition of the Holy Scriptures in the English language. Congress requested that its two chaplains, William White and George Duffield, examine the text, which they did. After receiving a positive report from them,

Congress provided the following endorsement for what is now known as "Aitken's Bible":

> That the United States in Congress assembled, highly approve the pious and laudable undertaking of Mr. Aitken, as subservient to the interest of religion, as well as an instance of the progress of arts in this country, and being satisfied from the above report [by White and Duffield] of his care and accuracy in the execution of the work, they recommend this edition of the Bible to the inhabitants of the United States, and hereby authorize him to publish this recommendation in the manner he shall think proper.[63]

Congress, perennially short of funds, could not help fund the publication of this Bible, but the Pennsylvania legislature offered Aitken a 150-pound, interest-free loan to complete his work. Ten thousand copies of his Bible were printed with the congressional endorsement.[64]

Finally, members of Congress sometimes appealed to the Bible and Christian moral principle when debating public policy. For instance, Roger Sherman opposed a congressional committee's proposal to increase the maximum number of lashes allowed for military discipline from one hundred to five hundred. John Sullivan reported in a letter to George Washington that "though a Great Majority of Congress were for it, the question was lost . . . [due to] principles Laid down by Levitical Law strongly urged by Roger Sherman Esq. and Co."[65] Although the record does not specify it, Sherman's objection almost certainly stemmed from Deuteronomy 25:3: "Forty stripes he may give him, and not exceed: lest, if he should exceed, and beat him above these with many stripes, then thy brother should seem vile unto thee."

CHURCH-STATE RELATIONS
IN THE NEW REPUBLIC

Article I, Section 8, of the Constitution does not give Congress the power to directly promote religion or morality. Even if it did, many members of the First Federal Congress would have declined to do so, believing that any such legislation should come from state or local governments. But within its constitutional powers, Congress and the other branches of the federal government did not hesitate to encourage Christian practices. As with state and earlier national officials, there is little evidence that they desired the strict separation of church and state.

Particularly relevant for interpreting the First Amendment are the actions of the First Congress, the body that drafted and proposed this constitutional provision. One of Congress's first acts was to appoint congressional chaplains.[66] Shortly after doing so, it reauthorized the Northwest Ordinance, which, as noted earlier, held that "religion, morality, and knowledge being necessary to good government and the happiness of mankind, schools and the means of education shall forever be encouraged."[67] And, to the surprise of no one except today's separationists, Congress agreed to pay congressional and military chaplains.[68]

On the day after the House approved the final wording of the Bill of Rights, Elias Boudinot, a founding member and the first president of the American Bible Society, proposed that Congress ask the president to recommend a day of public thanksgiving and prayer. In response to objections by Aedenus Burke and Thomas Tucker that those practices mimicked European customs and that such calls were properly issued by states, Roger Sherman justified the practice of thanksgiving, on any signal event, not only as a laudable one in itself, but as warranted by a number of precedents in holy writ: for instance, the solemn thanksgivings and rejoicings which took place in the time of Solomon, after the building of the temple, was a case in point. This example, he thought, worthy of Christian imitation on the present occasion; and he would agree with the gentleman who moved the resolution.[69]

Note that Sherman explicitly appealed to the Bible (i.e., "holy writ") to defend the practice of civic leaders encouraging citizens to pray. The House approved the motion and appointed Boudinot, Sherman, and Peter Silvester of New York to a committee to meet with senators about the matter. The Senate concurred with the House, and Congress requested that President Washington issue his famous 1789 Thanksgiving Proclamation. The text of his proclamation is worth quoting at some length:

Whereas it is the duty of all nations to acknowledge the providence of Almighty God, to obey His will, to be grateful for His benefits, and humbly to implore His protection and favor . . .

I do recommend and assign Thursday the 26th day of November next to be devoted by the people of these states to the service of that great and glorious Being, who is the beneficent Author of all the good that was, that is, or that will be—That we may then all unite in rendering unto Him our sincere and humble thanks—for His kind care and protection of the people of this country previous to their becoming a nation—for the signal and manifold mercies, and the favorable interpositions of His Providence which we experienced in the course and conclusion of the late war—for the great degree of tranquility, union, and plenty, which we have since enjoyed—for the peaceable and rational manner, in which we have been enabled to establish constitutions of government for our safety and happiness, and particularly the national one now lately instituted—for the civil and religious liberty with which we are blessed; and the means we have of acquiring and diffusing useful knowledge; and in general for all the great and various favors which He hath been pleased to confer upon us.

And also that we may then unite in most humbly offering our prayers and supplications to the great Lord and Ruler of Nations and beseech Him to pardon our national and other transgressions—to enable us all, whether in public or private stations, to perform our several and relative duties properly and punctually—to render our national government a blessing to all the people, by constantly being a government of wise, just, and constitutional laws, discreetly and faithfully executed and obeyed—to protect and guide all sovereigns and nations (especially such as have shewn kindness unto us) and to bless them with good government, peace, and concord—To promote the knowledge and practice of true religion and virtue, and the increase of science among them and us—and generally to grant unto all mankind such a degree of temporal prosperity as He alone knows to be best.[70]

Significantly, Washington emphasized the *duty* of nations to "obey" God, the necessity of beseeching Him "to pardon our national and other transgression," and his desire to promote "*true* religion and virtue" (emphasis added). Washington clearly did not think it inappropriate for the chief executive to encourage his fellow citizens to pray and to recognize the importance of faith.

"So Help Me God"

Separationists often think it significant that there is no con-temporary account of Washington saying "so help me God" when he took the oath of office.[71] But they often neglect to mention that he insisted on taking the oath on a Bible (which he kissed after taking the oath, a common practice well into the twentieth century) and that he, along with members of Congress and other dignitaries, proceeded to Saint Paul's church after the ceremony for prayer.[72] The Constitution does not include the words "so help me God" in its oath provisions, but virtually every state required them in their prescribed oaths. With few exceptions, the oaths for civic and military office that Washington took throughout his many years of service did as well.[73] It would have been unremarkable for Washington to add the words "so help me God" to his oath, but shocking to many if he neglected them. So it is eminently reasonable to infer from the lack of records that he added these words.[74]

Throughout his long career in politics, John Adams repeatedly spoke of the importance of religion and morality. And his actions, at both the state and the national level, make it evident that he thought civic officials should encourage religious beliefs and practices. In his presidential calls for prayer and fasting, he followed his predecessor in acknowledging Providence, the duty to worship God, and the necessity of citizens to confess their individual and collective sins. And he clearly referenced Jesus Christ (the "Redeemer of the world") and the third person of the Trinity:

> I have therefore thought fit to recommend . . . that all religious congregations do, with the deepest humility, acknowledge before God the manifold sins and transgressions with which we are justly chargeable as individuals and as a nation, beseeching Him at the same time, of His infinite grace, through the Redeemer of the world, freely to remit all our offenses, and to incline us by His Holy Spirit to that sincere repentance and reformation which may afford us reason to hope for his inestimable favor and heavenly benediction.[75]

Similarly, in a 1799 proclamation, he recommended another day to be

> observed throughout the United States of America as a day of solemn humiliation, fasting, and prayer; that the citizens on that day abstain as far as may be from their secular occupations, devote the time to the sacred duties of religion in public and in private; that they call to mind our numerous offenses against the Most High God, confess them before Him with the sincerest penitence, implore His pardoning mercy, through the Great Mediator and Redeemer, for our past transgressions, and that through the grace of His Holy Spirit we may be disposed and enabled to yield a more suitable obedience to His righteous requisitions in time to come; that He would interpose to arrest the progress of that impiety and licentiousness in principle and practice so offensive to Himself and so ruinous to mankind; that He would make us deeply sensible that "righteousness exalteth a nation:

but sin is a reproach to any people" [Prov. 14:34]; that He would turn us from our transgressions and turn His displeasure from us; that He would withhold us from unreasonable discontent, from disunion, faction, sedition, and insurrection.[76]

It is hardly unusual that Adams would appeal to Proverbs 14:34, which was, according to Daniel L. Dreisbach, one of the founders' favorite verses.[77] Critics of religion in the public square sometimes point out that Adams's proclamations were drafted by others.[78] This may be true, but it is also irrelevant. Many presidential speeches, proclamations, and addresses are drafted by trusted advisors. The president is responsible for who he asks to draft them and, more importantly, what he says or allows to be issued in his name. The proclamations quoted above leave no doubt that Adams thought it appropriate for presidents to issue robustly Christian calls for prayer and fasting.[79]

In 1962, the US Supreme Court declared teacher-led prayer in public schools to be unconstitutional.[80] It is ironic that when justices heard oral arguments in this case, the day's session opened with the prayer, "God save the United States and this Honorable Court." The first recorded instance of the Supreme Court opening with this prayer was in 1827, but federal circuit courts were opening with prayer as early as 1800. For instance, according to a New Hampshire paper:

> After the Jury were empaneled, the Judge delivered a most elegant and appropriate Charge . . . *Religion and Morality* were pleasingly inculcated and enforced, as being necessary to good government, good order and good laws, for "when the righteous are in authority, the people rejoice" [Prov. 29:2]. . . .

> After the Charge was delivered, the Rev. Mr. [Timothy] Alden addressed the Throne of Grace [Heb. 4:16], in an excellent, well adapted prayer.[81] (emphasis original)

Throughout the early republic, presidents, members of Congress, and federal justices promoted religion and morality in official and unofficial ways. A few founders, it is true, objected to some practices (e.g., Jefferson and presidential calls for prayer), but these were exceptions, not the rule.

BUT WHAT ABOUT THE BENEFIT OF CLERGY AND THE TREATY OF TRIPOLI?

In 1790, Congress passed a law entitled "An Act for the Punishment of Certain Crimes Against the United States."[82] Separationists who are not familiar with legal history like to point out that this statute stipulates that "the benefit of clergy shall not be used or allowed" in federal death penalty cases. Philosopher James F. Harris explains that

> since the earliest colonial days, when charged with a crime, clergy in the various colonies had been given the special privilege of standing trial in an ecclesiastical court instead of a civil court like ordinary citizens. This provision was removed by Congress for federal crimes committed against the United States. Such provisions for "benefit of clergy" were to remain in some states' laws for decades.[83]

Harris is correct that at one time "benefit of clergy" permitted ministers to be tried in ecclesiastical courts, but that time was the medieval era! In England, ecclesiastical courts lost jurisdiction over all criminal matters in 1576, but the benefit of clergy evolved into a tool that allowed first-time offenders—clergy and non-clergy alike—to avoid the death penalty in some cases. America *never* had ecclesiastical courts that substituted for secular courts, and ministers here *never* enjoyed the sorts of privilege that Harris thinks they did. Congress's action had absolutely nothing to do with religion; it simply made it clear that an archaic legal practice had no place in federal criminal law.

Perhaps no single document is as beloved by those who would deny that America had a Christian founding as America's 1797 treaty with Tripoli. The eleventh article of the treaty stipulates:

> As the government of the United States of America is not, in any sense, founded on the Christian religion; as it has in itself no character of enmity against the laws, religion or tranquility of Mussulmen; and, as the said States never have entered into any war, or act of hostility against any Mahometan nation, it is declared by the parties, that no pretext, arising from religious opinions, shall ever produce an interruption of the harmony existing between the two countries.[84]

Brooke Allen wrote that the "1797 Treaty of Tripoli illustrates the triumph . . . of Madisonian separationism."[85] Others, including professors James Harris, Frank Lambert, Richard Hughes, Martha Nussbaum, and Gregg Frazer, cite the treaty as evidence that America did not have a Christian founding.[86] Yet, when viewed in its historical context, there are very good reasons for not reading the article as a principled statement of church-state relations.

After the American colonies broke from Great Britain, the British navy ceased to protect American merchants in the Mediterranean Sea. American ships were captured often, and American citizens enslaved or taken hostage by pirates based in North Africa. In 1786, John Adams and Thomas Jefferson had the opportunity to ask Tripoli's ambassador why his nation attacked countries "who had done them no injury." The ambassador responded that it was because of "laws of their Prophet, that it was written in their Koran."[87] A decade later, Joel Barlow negotiated a treaty intended to protect American shipping in the region. President Adams sent the treaty to the US Senate, where it was ratified unanimously with no reported discussion.

Viewed in its international context, it seems most reasonable to view the eleventh article of the Treaty of Tripoli as a practical measure intended to bring peace with an Islamic power, rather than as an abstract statement of church-state relations. If this provision had been seen as the latter, surely some senators and members of the general public would have objected. Yet, even though the treaty was published in several newspapers, I am unaware of anyone objecting to it at the time.[88] Moreover, the treaty was renegotiated several times, and subsequent versions did not contain the article. The Barbary pirates remained a threat into the nineteenth century, although the United States' negotiating position improved after President Jefferson sent the US Marines to the "shores of Tripoli."[89]

It is not unreasonable for advocates of a secular founding to quote and highlight the Treaty of Tripoli. Indeed, it is one of the few documents from the era that offers some support for their position. However, when viewed in its historical context and in the face of the large amount of evidence presented in this book that America had a Christian founding, the document itself cannot support the claims made for it.

THEN WHY OPPOSE ESTABLISHMENTS?

After independence, most states either disestablished their churches (especially states where the Church of England was previously established) or moved to a system of "plural" or "multiple" establishments. In either case, debates were usually framed in terms of which arrangement would help true religion to flourish. In 1785, for instance, the Maryland House of Delegates proposed a general assessment bill that began with the following resolution:

> That in the opinion of this house, that the happiness of the people, and the good order and preservation of civil government, depend upon morality, religion, and piety; and that these cannot be generally diffused through a community, but by the *public* worship of Almighty God.[90] (emphasis original)

Similarly, in Virginia, a legislative committee headed by Patrick Henry drafted a general assessment bill that would have provided support to ministers from different denominations. Clergy should be supported by the government, the committee averred, because "the general diffusion of Christian knowledge hath a natural tendency to correct the morals of men, restrain their vices, and preserve the peace of society."[91] In Virginia, a supporter of Henry's general assessment bill contended in the *Virginia Gazette*, "It is an opinion confirmed by the united suffrage of the thinking part of mankind in all former ages; 'that the *general belief* and *public acknowledgment* of the great principles of religion are necessary to secure the order and happiness of society'"[92] (emphasis original).

The General Assembly received approximately ninety petitions supporting and opposing this bill, *none of which denied the importance of Christianity*; the only debated question was whether state support would help or hurt religion. Consider, for instance, two petitions from Westmoreland County that arrived at the Virginia General Assembly on the same day—November 2, 1784. The first supported Henry's bill, arguing that "religion is absolutely requisite for the well ordering of society," and that state subsidies are necessary to keep salaries high enough to attract the best candidates into the ministry.[93]

Evangelical opponents of the plan, on the other hand, were adamant that assessments were against "the spirit of the Gospel," that "the Holy Author of our Religion" did not require state support, and that Christianity was far purer before "Constantine first established Christianity by human laws."[94] In rejecting their fellow petitioners' arguments that government support was necessary to attract good candidates to the ministry, they argued that clergy should

> manifest to the world "that they are inwardly moved by the Holy Ghost to take upon them that Office," that they seek the good of Mankind and not worldly Interest. Let their doctrines be scriptural and their Lives upright. Then shall Religion (if departed) speedily return, and Deism be put to open shame, and its dreaded Consequences removed.[95]

In his famous Memorial, written in the same context, Madison argued that "ecclesiastical establishments, instead of maintaining the purity and efficacy of religion, have had a contrary operation, . . . [and] the bill is adverse to the diffusion of the light of Christianity."[96] Freeing Christianity from state control, he explained, would lead it to flourish, which would in turn "establish more firmly the liberties, the prosperity, and the happiness of the Commonwealth."[97] Henry's bill was defeated, and in its place, Madison convinced the assembly to enact Jefferson's "Bill for Establishing Religious Freedom," which likewise proclaimed that "all attempts to influence [the mind] by temporal punishments, or burthens, or by civil incapacitations, tend only to beget habits of hypocrisy and meanness, and are a departure from the plan of the holy author of our religion."[98]

CONCLUSION

America's founders did not want a national church, and many were coming to oppose establishments at the state level as well. Yet, without an exception of which I am aware, they agreed with George Washington that of "all the dispositions and habits which lead to political prosperity, religion and morality are indispensable supports."[99] Moreover, they all acted as if civic authorities should promote and encourage religion and morality, even if some later came to question the appropriateness of doing so (e.g., Madison in his "Detached Memoranda"). There was no support for contemporary visions of a separation of church and state that would have political leaders avoid religious language and require public spaces to be stripped of religious symbols. The assertion that the founders desired to build a high and impregnable wall of separation between church and state is, to put it bluntly, pure fantasy.

An originalist understanding of the First Amendment permits the national and state governments to promote religion, and even to specifically encourage and support Christianity. But that does not mean they should do so today. America is far more diverse than it was in the eighteenth century, and our civic leaders represent all citizens. So political prudence and civic friendship suggest that it is best for presidents and other civic leaders to use language that unites rather than divides Americans. And when legislatures choose to make benefits available to religious organizations, they should not discriminate among religious communities, so long as these groups are qualified to receive them. With all of this, the historical record is clear: in no manner did the founders conceive of a government from which religion—Christianity above all—was precluded. In fact, the founders believed it is necessary for the two to be intermingled and mutually supportive.

SUGGESTIONS FOR FURTHER READING

Curry, Thomas J. *The First Freedoms: Church and State in America to the Passage of the First Amendment*. New York: Oxford University Press, 1986. A fine overview of church-state relations in early America.

Drakeman, Donald L. *Church, State, and Original Intent*. New York: Cambridge University Press, 2010. A well-researched volume demonstrating that many jurists and scholars have distorted the founding generation's understanding of the Establishment Clause.

Hutson, James H. *Church and State in America: The First Two Centuries*. New York: Cambridge University Press, 2008. An excellent, concise account of the development of religious liberty and church-state relations in early America.

Olasky, Marvin. *Fighting for Liberty and Virtue: Political and Cultural Wars in Eighteenth-Century America*. Wheaton: Crossway Books, 1995. Helps demonstrate that the founders were motivated by religious and moral concerns, and that they were willing to utilize governments to protect and promote faith and virtue.

CHAPTER 5

Christianity,
Religious
Liberty, and
Religious
Exemptions

Inspired by Enlightenment ideas of free inquiry, Jefferson used his reason to argue that government ought to have nothing to do with religious matters other than to guarantee religious liberty.

FRANK LAMBERT, SEPARATION OF CHURCH AND STATE

Religious toleration generally arose from the Enlightenment.

DAVID L. HOLMES, THE FAITHS OF THE FOUNDING FATHERS

The theistic rationalism of the key Founders made it natural and easy for them to grant religious liberty. By contrast, it would be difficult for those who believe in the importance of fundamental doctrines and a specific road to Heaven (such as the Puritans in seventeenth-century New England) to allow "false" or "blasphemous" religions to be practiced within their sphere of authority.

GREGG FRAZER, THE RELIGIOUS BELIEFS OF AMERICA'S FOUNDERS

In its conception and language, the [Virginia] Statute and the First Amendment were Enlightenment creations.

JON BUTLER, "COERCION, MIRACLE, REASON"[1]

The framing generation believed that conduct, even when religiously motivated, could be regulated by the state in the interest of others.

MARCI A. HAMILTON, GOD VS. THE GAVEL

There should not be exemptions to general laws with neutral purposes, unless those exemptions do not shift burdens or risks onto others.

BRIAN LEITER, WHY TOLERATE RELIGION?[2]

S cholars routinely assert that the Enlightenment inspired civic leaders in the West to adopt religious liberty. They came to value reason over revelation, and so concluded that it is irrational to kill or persecute in the name of God. Enlightenment ideas had some positive influence (especially in Europe), but in this chapter I contend that an important reason Americans embraced religious liberty was because of their Christian convictions. Biblical and theological arguments played key roles in defining and supporting what many founders called "the sacred rights of conscience." I briefly consider developments in the pre-founding era, but focus on arguments for freedom of conscience made in the late eighteenth century. In addition to supporting freedom of worship, many founders believed that citizens should be free to act according to their religious convictions, unless the government has a compelling reason to prevent them from doing so. Moreover, most of America's founders thought the religious liberty of all citizens should be protected, even those who did not share the majority's faith.

WHY RELIGIOUS LIBERTY?

According to some, a faith commitment necessitates that one be intolerant of other religions or sects. From AD 325, when Emperor

Constantine called the Council of Nicaea to resolve a theological debate, to the founding of the American colonies, it was common for civic authorities to promote what they considered to be true religion. This often included discriminating against or even persecuting those who deviated from the rulers' understanding of Christian orthodoxy. America's earliest colonial leaders, from north to south, were not immune to this temptation. The extent to which colonial authorities oppressed religious minorities is often exaggerated. Even in Puritan New England, civic authorities did not try to compel belief, and orderly dissenters were tolerated. However, disorderly dissenters like Anne Hutchinson and Roger Williams were not; and, on rare occasion, a *very* disorderly dissenter, such as the Quaker Mary Dyer, was executed.

Fortunately, or providentially, between the establishment of the early colonies and the founding era, the way Americans approached religious liberty changed in important ways. This happened for several reasons. At a practical level, almost from the start, despite a desire for homogeneity, America attracted diverse groups of immigrants from England and continental Europe. From an early date, even in Congregational New England and the Anglican South, there were dissenters, and the middle colonies were always a muddle. A great illustration of this is a 1771 woodcut of the skyline of New York City. Of the twenty-one buildings identified, most are houses of worship, including those belonging to Presbyterians, Anglicans, Dutch Calvinists, Moravians, Jews, Quakers, Anabaptists, Catholics, Methodists, and others. Admittedly, New York was a particularly diverse city, but there was significant pluralism in each colony. This diversity forced civic authorities to negotiate laws and policies encouraging different groups to get along (sometimes with more success than others).

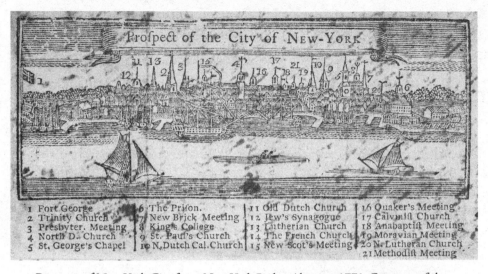

Prospect of New York City from *New York Pocket Almanac*, 1771. Courtesy of the American Antiquarian Society.

The lot of religious minorities in America improved markedly in the eighteenth century. These advances were aided by parliamentary legislation; pragmatic attempts by civic leaders to deal with religious diversity; and biblical, practical, and theoretical arguments for the liberty of conscience made by indisputably pious men, such as Roger Williams, William Penn, Elisha Williams, Samuel Davies, Isaac Backus, and John Leland. These Christian leaders advocated religious liberty for a variety of reasons, including the conviction that persecution does not work, that liberty of conscience causes true religion to flourish, and that the Bible and Christian theology require religious freedom.[3]

Let's begin by considering the fact that religious persecution doesn't work. Far from being a merely prudential argument, the chief concern of critics was that persecution hindered the flourishing of true Christianity. William Penn, for instance, contended in 1675 that "force makes hypocrites, 'tis persuasion only that makes converts."[4] He reiterated this conviction a dozen years later, noting that persecution "converts no body; it may breed *hypocrisy*, that is quite another thing than *salvation*"[5] (emphasis original). Good social and legal policies should produce faithful Christians, not hypocrites.

When religious minorities gain political power, they sometimes forget their commitment to religious liberty. But when Penn had the opportunity to craft laws for Pennsylvania, he included a provision in the colony's statutes that said:

> All persons living in this province, who confess and acknowledge the one Almighty and eternal God, to be the Creator, Upholder and Ruler of the world; and that hold themselves obliged in conscience to live peaceably and justly in civil society, shall, in no ways, be molested or prejudiced for their religious persuasion, or practice, in matters of faith and worship, nor shall they be compelled, at any time, to frequent or maintain any religious worship, place or ministry whatever.[6]

Penn may be criticized for guaranteeing religious liberty only for monotheists, but in his defense, there is no record of any citizen of Pennsylvania being anything other than a monotheist until well after he died. Although some Native Americans in the region might be characterized as polytheists, no colony dealt more fairly with and used less force against indigenous peoples than did Pennsylvania.[7] Penn thought that religious liberty helped Christianity flourish, and he was also convinced that it promoted virtue, stability, and even trade.[8]

Arguments similar to Penn's were adopted by numerous Americans in the eighteenth century. For instance, the Baptist minister Isaac Backus contended in 1773 that where each person, and each society, are equally protected from being injured by others, all enjoying equal liberty, to attend and support the worship which they believe is right, having no more striving for mastery or superiority than little children (which we must all come to, or not *enter into the kingdom of* heaven [Matt. 18:3]) how happy are its effects in civil society?[9] (emphasis original)

As an evangelist, Backus cared more about the eternal state of souls than worldly happiness, but like most founders, he also understood that true religion was good for society.

In Massachusetts, the pseudonymous author Worcestriensis opposed compulsion in matters of faith because, "instead of making men religious, [it] generally has a contrary tendency, it works not to conviction, but most naturally leads them to hypocrisy."[10] The author had no doubt that religion was beneficial to civil society, and he did not even oppose state "encouragement of the GENERAL PRINCIPLES of religion and morality"; he rejected compulsion primarily because it did not work.[11]

In 1776, the Presbyterians of Hanover County, Virginia, sent a memorial to the General Assembly where they argued that

if mankind were left in the quiet possession of their unalienable religious privileges, Christianity, as in the days of the Apostles, would continue to prevail and flourish in the greatest purity, by its own native excellence, and under the all-disposing providence of God.[12]

These believers made a variety of arguments in favor of religious liberty, and against religious establishments. But like virtually everyone advocating these positions, their key contention was that religious liberty causes Christianity to flourish *and* to be purer. In like manner, the future Supreme Court Justice James Iredell remarked in North Carolina's Ratifying Convention that it

> would be happy for mankind if religion was permitted to take its own course, and maintain itself by the excellence of its own doctrines. The divine Author of our religion never wished for its support by world authority. Has he not said that the gates of hell shall not prevail against it [Matt. 16:18]? It made much greater progress for itself, than when supported by the greatest authority upon earth.[13]

During the height of the First Great Awakening, Elisha Williams, a Congregationalist minister, Yale rector, member of the General Assembly, and judge on the Connecticut Superior Court, wrote an impassioned plea for religious liberty entitled "The Essential Rights and Liberties of Protestants" (1744). A central contention in this work is

> that the sacred scriptures are the alone rule of faith and practice to a Christian, all Protestants are agreed in; and must therefore inviolably maintain, that every Christian has a *right of judging for himself* what he is to believe and practice in religion according to that rule.[14] (emphasis original)

Williams's argument encapsulates some of the key commitments of the Protestant Reformation—notably, *sola scriptura* and the priesthood of all believers. If one truly believes these doctrines, Williams averred, one must embrace freedom of conscience. To be sure, this is a very Protestant argument, and so might not have been as effective in Catholic countries. But in a colony that was 99.99 percent Protestant, it worked well.

Williams made other arguments, including what has become a

famous appeal (at least among academic students of the founding) to John Locke's social compact.[15] But after citing Locke, he returned to his Protestant arguments, noting that everyone "is under an indispensable obligation to search the Scriptures for himself (which contains the whole of it) and to make the best use of it he can for his own information in the will of GOD, the nature and duties of Christianity." He moved quickly from this restatement of the argument to the conclusion that "the rights of conscience are sacred and equal in all, and strictly speaking unalienable."[16]

Freedom of conscience was so important that it was common for it to be referred to as a "sacred right." For example, when the Continental Congress wrote instructions to commissioners appointed to Canada in 1776, they included the following charge: "You are further to declare, that we hold sacred the rights of conscience, and may promise to the whole people, solemnly in our name, the free and undisturbed exercise of their religion."[17] Likewise, President James Madison's July 23, 1813, call for prayer connects the "sacred rights of conscience" to our "present happiness [and] . . . future hopes."[18]

One of the most important founding-era arguments in favor of religious liberty was based on the theological principle that humans have a duty to worship God as their consciences dictate. A fine example of this is George Mason's 1776 draft of Article XVI of Virginia's Declaration of Rights, which reads:

> That as religion, or the duty which we owe to our divine and omnipotent Creator, and the manner of discharging it, can be governed only by reason and conviction, not by force or violence; and therefore that all men should enjoy the fullest toleration in the exercise of religion, according to the dictates of conscience, unpunished and unrestrained by the magistrate.[19]

This draft was reprinted throughout the states, and it had an important impact on subsequent state constitutions and the national Bill of Rights—but an important alteration was made before it became law. James Madison, in his first significant public act, objected to the use of "toleration" in the article, presumably because he thought it implied that religious liberty was a grant from the state that could be revoked. The Virginia Convention agreed, and Article XVI was amended to make it clear that "the free exercise of religion" is a right, not a privilege granted by the state.[20]

In Massachusetts, the Baptist minister Isaac Backus appealed to Matthew 22:21, when he argued that Christians "must render unto Caesar the things that are his, but that it is of as much importance not to render unto him anything that belongs to God."[21] Worship belongs to God alone, so Christians must be free to worship Him according to the dictates of their consciences, not as directed by the state.[22] Several years later, a Baptist elder Noah Alden asked him how a "bill of rights ought to be drawn." Among Backus's suggestions was a religious liberty provision that reads:

> As God is the only worthy object of all religious worship, and nothing can be true religion but a voluntary obedience unto His revealed will, of which each rational soul has an equal right to judge for itself, every person has an unalienable right to act in all religious affairs according to the full persuasion of his own mind, where others are not injured thereby.[23]

His fellow Baptist minister John Leland made a similar argument in his important pamphlet *The Rights of Conscience Inalienable* (1791).[24]

For a final example, let's return to the Massachusetts Constitution of

1780, drafted in part by John Adams and ratified by an overwhelmingly Congregationalist electorate. Article II of the constitution proclaims:

> It is the right as well as the duty of all men in society, publicly and at stated seasons, to worship the Supreme Being, the great Creator and Preserver of the universe. And no subject shall be hurt, molested, or restrained, in his person, liberty, or estate, for worshipping God in the manner and season most agreeable to the dictates of his own conscience, or for his religious profession or sentiments, provided he doth not disturb the public peace or obstruct others in their religious worship.[25]

America's founders routinely made arguments grounded on Christian premises to support a robust understanding of religious liberty.[26]

By the end of the revolutionary era, every state offered significant protection of religious liberty.[27] The federal Constitution did not contain a religious liberty provision, only because its supporters believed the national government did not have the delegated power to pass laws interfering with religious belief or practice.[28] In the face of popular outcry, the First Congress proposed, and the states ratified, a constitutional amendment stating that "Congress shall make no law respecting an establishment of religion, or prohibiting the free exercise thereof."[29]

WHAT DOES THE FREE EXERCISE CLAUSE PROTECT? OR, WHAT SHOULD HAPPEN TO BARRONELLE STUTZMAN?

Today, almost no American is against religious liberty per se. Arguments begin when a person's religious convictions conflict with general laws or policies aimed at advancing the common good. These statutes rarely mention specific religions or religious practices, but they nonetheless prevent some citizens from acting on their religious convictions (or make it very costly for them to do so). Objections arise, for example, when religious pacifists ask to be exempted from military service; Amish citizens desire their teenagers to be excused from mandatory school attendance laws; or photographers, florists, and bakers decline to participate in wedding ceremonies to which they have religious objections.[30]

America's founders were well aware of these sorts of conflicts, and they developed eminently reasonable solutions for them. If the law in question promotes the common good, and thus should not simply be repealed, their solution was to craft religious exemptions or accommodations to protect religious citizens. This approach allows the state to achieve important policy objectives without forcing people to act against their sincerely held religious beliefs. Of course, not every conviction can be accommodated, but jurists and scholars have developed useful tests to determine which convictions should be protected, as discussed below.[31]

Consider the case of Barronelle Stutzman, who has worked as a florist in Richland, Washington, for more than thirty-five years. For nine years, she willingly served Rob Ingersoll and his same-sex partner, well aware of the nature of their relationship. On multiple occasions, she created floral arrangements to help them celebrate anniversaries, birthdays, and so on. In 2012, she heard through an employee that Mr. Ingersoll was going to ask her to provide flowers for his wedding ceremony. She talked it over with her husband and concluded,

> My faith teaches me that marriage is between one man and one woman. Marriage is a sacred covenant between a man and a woman, as Christ is to the church. To create and design something from my

heart that helps celebrate their marriage would be dishonoring to God, and my convictions.[32]

When Mr. Ingersoll came to the store with his request, she gently declined to create a floral arrangement for him, gave him a hug, and referred him to a florist who had no such objections. In a world of free and responsible citizens, that should have been the end of it. Instead, Washington's attorney general and the ACLU hit her with ruinous lawsuits that may drive her out of business. The Supreme Court of the state of Washington has ruled against her, but the case is being appealed.[33] Regardless of how this case is decided, debates over accommodations are bound to continue. The founders' approach to these problems offers valuable insight that should inform future public policy.

What is often missing from public discussions of issues like these is an acknowledgment that it is possible for legislators to craft exemptions to neutral laws *and* still meet important policy goals. This was certainly the view of America's founders, as this chapter demonstrates. By the mid-twentieth century, these solutions had become well established in American law. However, since the turn of the century, an increasing number of "progressive" jurists, politicians, and academics have turned their backs on the founders' commitment to protecting the sacred rights of conscience. This is a mistake.

RELIGIOUS ACCOMMODATIONS IN THE FOUNDING ERA

Government was far less intrusive in eighteenth-century America. Most state legal codes were published in one volume, and the national government passed few laws directly affecting individuals. But there were two major policy areas where religious citizens sometimes ran afoul of general, neutrally applicable laws: oath requirements and military service. Oaths were considered important for ensuring that citizens were loyal, that witnesses tell the truth in judicial proceedings, and that public officials would serve the common good rather than their own self-interest. And military service—at the local, state, and national levels—was necessary for protecting life, liberty, and property.

Oath Requirements

Historically, oaths have been seen as essential for ensuring the loyalty and fidelity of citizens and elected officials. They were also viewed as critically important for the effective functioning of judicial systems. As noted earlier, in his farewell address, President George Washington asked, "Where is the security for property, for reputation, for life, if the sense of religious obligation *desert* the oaths, which are the instruments of investigation in courts of justice?"[34] (emphasis original). The state obviously has an interest in the loyalty of its citizens and in having a reliable judicial system, and oaths were viewed as a crucial means of securing such.[35] In the Christian West, oaths usually invoke God as the witness of the oath taker's veracity, and they almost always concluded with the phrase "so help me God."

Most citizens do not object to swearing oaths, but members of the Society of Friends, more commonly known as Quakers, refused to do so as early as the 1640s. Simply put, they took (and take) biblical passages literally, such as Matthew 5:33–37, where Jesus said: "Swear not at all. . . . But let your communication be, Yea, yea; Nay, nay: for whatsoever is more than these cometh of evil." They interpret these passages quite strictly, refusing to "swear" oaths but willing to "affirm" or otherwise assent to them. In England, they were routinely jailed for failing to swear oaths and, after the Glorious Revolution of 1688, for refusing to swear oaths promising loyalty to the new regime. In 1696, Parliament passed a law known as the Quaker Act, which allowed Friends in England to offer a "Solemn Affirmation or Declaration that 'I A.B. do declare in the Presence of Almighty God the Witness of the Truth of what I say'" in some cases. But Quakers still faced numerous disabilities. For instance, they were not permitted to be witnesses in criminal cases or hold civic offices because of their unwillingness to swear oaths. In England, they, and others with conscientious scruples against swearing, were not able to testify in criminal trials until 1828, or become members of Parliament until 1832.[36]

American colonial governments were not originally bound by the Quaker Act, but many voluntarily accommodated Quakers and others who objected to swearing oaths. Notably, in 1647—almost half a century before Parliament passed the act—Rhode Island enacted a law to protect the "consciences of sundry men, . . . [who] may scruple the giving or taking of an oath." Instead of swearing, these individuals were permitted to offer a "solemn profession or testimony in a court of record" so they could hold office or give testimony.[37] This remarkably generous accommodation was available to anyone (not just Quakers). It is all the more striking because the colony's founder, Roger Williams, detested Quakers.[38]

By the early eighteenth century, most colonies voluntarily accommodated Quakers and others who had objections to swearing oaths, and as the century progressed, Parliament and royal officials sometimes encouraged or even required them to do so. After America broke with Great Britain, state governments could have revoked these laws and policies, but none of them did. Moreover, when America's founders gathered in Philadelphia to draft a new constitution, they wove accommodations into the nation's fundamental law. Articles I, II, and VI permit individuals to either swear *or affirm* oaths. The best known of these provisions is Article II, Section 1, which reads, "Before he [the president] enter on the execution of his office, he shall take the following oath or affirmation: 'I do solemnly swear, (or affirm,) that I will faithfully execute . . .'" Of course, one does not need to be religious to take advantage of these provisions. But in the context in which they were written, there is little doubt that these accommodations were intended for Quakers and others who had religious objections to taking oaths.

THE PRESIDENTIAL OATH OF OFFICE

America's two Quaker presidents, Herbert Hoover and Richard Nixon, each swore the oath of office. Franklin Pierce, who was president from 1853 to 1857, opted to affirm rather than swear, although he was not a member of a denomination that opposed swearing oaths. Some commentators believe his decision had something to do with the tragic death of his eleven-year-old son two months before he was inaugurated, but there is little evidence to support this hypothesis.[39] Pierce, like John Quincy Adams before him, also elected to take the oath with his hand on a law book rather than a Bible. But the vast majority of presidents have taken their oaths on Bibles; often opened to specific passages meaningful to them.[40]

136

One might have thought the adoption of an inclusive Constitution would have made it clear that citizens who object to swearing oaths would be protected (at least in the federal context). But even in the new republic, there were a few who would limit religious accommodations. A draft version of the Judiciary Act of 1789 permitted Quakers—but only Quakers—appearing before federal courts to affirm rather than swear oaths. Senator William Maclay of Pennsylvania proposed instead that "all persons conscientiously scrupulous of taking an oath" should be able to make an affirmation. To support his argument, he appealed to the Constitution, which, in his words, does not "narrow the ground of conscience." The final version of the Judiciary Act permits anyone to affirm rather than swear an oath.[41]

America's founders were committed to accommodating citizens who have religious objections to swearing oaths. And these exemptions have only expanded, at both the state and national levels. There is no reason to believe that exempting Quakers and others from swearing oaths has had a detrimental effect on the judicial system, or that these citizens have been less loyal to America than other groups.

Military Service

Among the many responsibilities of the civil government, few are as important as national security. Virtually no one disputes that governments have an obligation to protect their citizens from external threats. In the modern era, nations have regularly relied on compulsory militia service or conscription to raise armies. Religious pacifists often ask to be excused from such service, yet many countries reject their pleas. Some American colonies and states have done this as well, but, at their best, civic leaders in America have opted to protect religious pacifists. Such accommodations are particularly noteworthy in the earliest colonies, as they were, upon occasion, literally faced with extermination at the hands of Native Americans and/or foreign powers.

During the War of Independence, Congress did not have the power to require service in the Continental army, and so most troops were raised by the states. Although its resolution had no binding power, Congress supported accommodating religious pacifists with the following July 18, 1775, proclamation:

> As there are some people, who, from religious principles, cannot bear arms in any case, this Congress intend no violence to their consciences, but earnestly recommend it to them, to contribute liberally in this time of universal calamity, to the relief of their distressed brethren in the several colonies, and to do all other services to their oppressed Country, which they can consistently with their religious principles.[42]

Most states agreed.

Fourteen years later, during the debates in the First Federal Congress over the Bill of Rights, James Madison proposed a version of what became the Second Amendment, which stipulated that "no person religiously scrupulous, shall be compelled to bear arms."[43] Although largely forgotten today, this provision provoked almost as much recorded debate as the First Amendment's religion provisions. James Jackson, a representative from Georgia, insisted that if such an accommodation were made, those protected should be required to hire substitutes. Roger Sherman objected that it "is well-known that those who are religiously scrupulous of bearing arms, are equally scrupulous of getting substitutes or paying an equivalent; many of them would rather die than do either one or the other."[44] Sherman's point is an important one, since pacifists objected regularly to the requirement that they pay someone to fight on their behalf, or to pay a fee to the state that could be used to hire someone.

Madison's proposal was approved by the House but rejected by the Senate, and it did not appear in the final text of what would become the Second Amendment. Madison returned to the issue two months later, as representatives debated a bill regulating the militia when called into national service. He offered an amendment to protect from militia service

> persons conscientiously scrupulous of bearing arms. *It is the glory of our country, said he, that a more sacred regard to the rights of mankind is preserved, than has heretofore been known.* The Quaker merits some attention on this delicate point, liberty of conscience. They had it in their own power to establish their religion by law, they did not. He was disposed to make the exception gratuitous, but supposed it impracticable.[45] (emphasis added)

The amended bill eventually passed, although with the requirement that conscientious objectors must hire a substitute.[46]

Madison's commitment to protecting religious citizens is noteworthy, even if the practical concern that protecting pacifists could undermine national security is understandable. States generally accommodated citizens who opposed war, as did the national government when it got into the conscription business in the twentieth century. Indeed, Congress eventually eliminated the requirement to hire a substitute (which, of course, favored the well-off over the poor), requiring instead that pacifists serve in noncombatant roles.[47]

Today, some academics and activists contend that religious accommodations violate the Establishment Clause.[48] As a matter of originalism, there is absolutely no reason to believe this is the case. The federal government had a very limited reach in the eighteenth century. But in those few areas where it enacted constitutional provisions, laws, or policies that could infringe upon the religious convictions of citizens, notably oaths and military service, America's founders created accommodations to protect them. Religious accommodations are clearly permissible as a matter of originalism—and they are, as well, good public policy.

APPLYING THE FOUNDERS' INSIGHTS TODAY

There is an extensive academic debate about whether or not an originalist interpretation of the Free Exercise Clause requires that governments craft exemptions to protect religious citizens.[49] I am sympathetic to the argument that it does, but one does not have to be an originalist to reach this conclusion. In the 1963 case of *Sherbert v. Verner*, the Supreme Court, in an opinion written by the liberal, non-originalist Justice William J. Brennan, adopted the rule that government actions that burden a religious practice must be justified by a compelling state interest.[50] Later, justices added the requirement that this interest must be pursued in the least restrictive manner possible. Collectively known as the "Sherbert Test," this approach provided excellent, although not perfect, protection for religious citizens.

Unfortunately, a majority of Supreme Court justices, led by the conservative Justice Antonin Scalia, repudiated this approach in *Oregon v. Smith*, 494 U.S. 872 (1990). The case involved Native Americans who believed they were obligated to use peyote (an illegal drug) in religious ceremonies. The Supreme Court ruled that the First Amendment did not require that the Native Americans be accommodated, but that legislatures *could* accommodate them. Both conservative and liberal citizens objected to the opinion. In response, Congress enacted the Religious Freedom Restoration Act (RFRA) of 1993 to restore the old Sherbert Test. It is noteworthy that the bill passed the House without a dissenting vote, was approved 97 to 3 by the Senate, and was signed into law by President Bill Clinton.

As an Oregonian, I am pleased to report that shortly after *Smith* was decided, the state legislature passed a statute protecting the right of individuals to use peyote in religious ceremonies. In 1994, without any recorded objections, Congress amended the American Indian Religious Freedom Act to protect Native Americans in the twenty-two states that did not permit them to use peyote in religious ceremonies. Some readers might object that there is a compelling interest in prohibiting people from using illegal drugs for any reason. This argument has merit, but in these cases, peyote is only used in small amounts and in *bona fide* (and ancient) religious ceremonies.[51] Permitting its use is similar to Congress allowing the use of "sacramental wine" for communion and other religious rituals during Prohibition.[52]

RELIGIOUS FREEDOM RESTORATION ACT

The Religious Freedom Restoration Act, known by its initials RFRA, was enacted to restore the old Sherbert Test. It stipulates that

> Government shall not substantially burden a person's exercise of religion even if the burden results from a rule of general applicability, . . . [except] if it demonstrates that application of the burden to the person [is] . . . in furtherance of a compelling governmental interest, . . . [and] is the least restrictive means of furthering that compelling governmental interest.[53]

The law was meant to apply to all levels of government, but in 1996, the Supreme Court ruled that it could not be applied to the states. In response, twenty-one states have enacted RFRAs of their own.[54]

In the 1990s, Republicans and Democrats were able to come together to protect religious liberty.[55] But, since the turn of the century, some jurists, politicians, scholars, and activists have abandoned the founders' commitment to accommodating religious citizens. For instance, in the academy, professors such as Marci Hamilton, Brian Leiter, John Corvino, Richard Schragger, and Micah Schwartzman have made well-publicized arguments attacking the logic and/or substance of accommodations that protect (or should protect) religious citizens from neutral, generally applicable laws.[56] Particularly worrisome is the contention that religion is not "special."[57]

In the political arena, the Obama administration showed little concern for religious liberty when it required businesses to provide contraceptives and abortifacients to employees, even when business owners had religious convictions against doing so.[58] In 2016, the US Commission on Civil Rights issued a report that said religious accommodations should be virtually nonexistent. The commission's chair, Martin R. Castro, remarked in his personal statement:

> The phrases "religious liberty" and "religious freedom" will stand
> for nothing except hypocrisy so long as they remain code words
> for discrimination, intolerance, racism, sexism, homophobia,
> Islamophobia, Christian supremacy or any form of intolerance.[59]

State civil rights commissions have been similarly dismissive of religious liberty concerns, and some have been downright hostile to people of faith. For instance, the Colorado Civil Rights Commission displayed such clear animus toward a Christian baker whose religious convictions did not allow him to bake a cake celebrating a same-sex wedding that Supreme Court justices ruled 7–2 in his favor in *Masterpiece Cakeshop v. Colorado Civil Rights Commission* (2018).[60]

The Trump administration has been friendlier to religious citizens than its predecessor, but cause for concern remains. President Trump's 2017 executive order, aimed at better protecting religious liberty, was described by ACLU executive director Anthony Romero as "an elaborate photo-op with no discernible policy outcome." He then went on to say that his organization would not bother to challenge it.[61] President

Trump has since taken additional steps to better protect religious liberty, but every executive action he has taken could be repealed by a subsequent administration.[62] Religious liberty should not depend on who is president.[63]

America's founders embraced a robust understanding of religious liberty—one that included creating exemptions to protect religious citizens from general, neutrally applicable laws. To return to the case of Barronelle Stutzman, let's assume for the sake of argument that states need laws banning discrimination on the basis of sexual orientation.[64] If these laws are beneficial, repealing them to protect Stutzman would harm the common good. But it does not follow that the state should drive her out of business because of her religious convictions. Instead, the state could accommodate Stutzman by permitting her (and others like her) to decline to participate in same-sex wedding ceremonies. Such an accommodation would not permit people who simply dislike homosexuals to refuse to serve them, and exemptions need not be granted for essential services such as medical care and police protection.[65]

I am well aware that this solution will raise objections from both sides. On the one hand, many conservatives think we should simply abolish laws prohibiting discrimination on the basis of sexual orientation. On the other hand, supporters of LGBTQ rights often oppose all religious accommodations in these matters. The reality is that we live in a pluralistic, diverse country. Like America's founders, we need to work together to figure out how the rights of all Americans can best be protected. Carefully crafted accommodations in these and other areas could protect religious citizens without hindering states from achieving important policy objectives.[66]

RELIGIOUS LIBERTY FOR ALL

Most citizens who have been protected by the Free Exercise Clause, or laws like the Religious Freedom Restoration Act, have been members of small religious groups that have little political power. For instance, Jehovah's Witnesses have been protected from being compelled to salute and pledge allegiance to the American flag,[67] Muslim prisoners have been permitted to grow beards despite regulations requiring inmates to be clean shaven,[68] members of a New Mexican branch of a Brazilian church have been allowed to use hallucinogenic tea in religious ceremonies,[69] and Amish families have been exempted from compulsory school attendance.[70]

The argument here is *not* that America's founders would have protected each of these minorities in these cases. It is that protecting the religious liberty of all citizens whenever possible is the logical application of their commitment to religious liberty. Quakers are Christians, but they were a tiny minority in eighteenth-century America, and many of their convictions were unpopular. Yet, as we have seen, America's founders made serious efforts to accommodate their religious commitments.

America's founders were profoundly influenced by Christianity, but they did not design a constitutional order only for fellow believers. This fact is understood by most civic leaders and jurists, but, alas, not everyone agrees. For instance, 28 percent of Americans favor a ban on building mosques in their communities, and some citizens argue that the First Amendment does not protect Muslims.[71] The founders explicitly prohibited religious tests for federal offices, and they understood that doing so would permit "a Papist or Infidel" or "pagans, deists, and

Mahometans" to be elected.[72] Some of them undoubtedly thought that these outcomes would not be ideal, but others may well have thought that it would be better to vote for, say, a reasonable, competent Jew than an irrational, incompetent Christian. Citizens are free to vote for or against a candidate because of his or her faith, but no one may properly deny their fellow Americans the ability to worship God and act according to the dictates of their consciences. It is fitting to conclude this chapter by returning to President Washington's eloquent letter to a tiny religious minority, where he proclaimed:

> All possess alike liberty or conscience and immunities of citizenship. It is now no more that toleration is spoken of, as if it was by the indulgence of one class of people, that another enjoyed the exercise of their inherent natural rights. For happily the Government of the United States, which gives to bigotry no sanction, to persecution no assistance requires only that they who live under its protection should demean themselves as good citizens, in giving it on all occasions their effectual support.[73]

All who would live up to the founders' ideal for freedom of conscience must insist that, except in the most extreme circumstances, every American has a right to live according to his or her religious convictions, no matter how unpopular they may be. This includes permitting florists not to participate in same-sex wedding ceremonies, Jehovah's Witnesses to refuse to salute the American flag, and Muslims to build mosques on the same terms that Christians build churches. The moment we start picking which convictions we choose to protect and which we do not, is the moment we abandon the founders' commitment to defending "the sacred rights of conscience."

SUGGESTIONS FOR
FURTHER READING

Eberstadt, Mary. *It's Dangerous to Believe.* New York: Harper, 2016. Helps document increasing threats to religious liberty in America, especially for citizens who hold traditional beliefs.

Hall, Mark David. "Religious Accommodations and the Common Good." *Heritage Foundation Backgrounder,* October 26, 2015, http://www .heritage.org/research/reports/2015/10/religiousaccommodations -and-the-common-good. An overview of how legislatures and courts have approached religious exemptions throughout American history.

Inazu, John D. *Confident Pluralism: Surviving and Thriving through Deep Difference.* Chicago: University of Chicago Press, 2016. An important argument in favor of pluralism and civility.

Murphy, Andrew R. *Conscience and Community: Revisiting Toleration and Religious Dissent in Early Modern England and America.* University Park: Penn State University Press, 2001. Contrary to many scholars, Murphy shows that religious arguments played an important role in the rise of religious liberty.

Soper, J. Christopher, Kevin R. den Dulk, and Stephen V. Monsma. *The Challenge of Pluralism: Church and State in Six Democracies,* 3rd ed. Lanham: Rowman & Littlefield, 2017. An excellent comparative study of religious liberty and church-state relations in America, Germany, England, Australia, Holland, and France.

CONCLUSION

I n this book I have presented a great deal of evidence that America had a Christian founding. If all it accomplishes is to provide a more complete account of Christianity's role in the American founding, I will consider it a success.[1] Progressive secularists may want to believe that most of America's founders were deists who created a "godless" Constitution that strictly separated church and state, but these views fly in the face of evidence. This book may change a few minds, and it should enable readers already skeptical of these arguments to better combat them.

But I hope this book does more than set the historical record straight. As mentioned in the introduction, there is much wisdom in James Wilson's observation that "of all governments, those are the best, which, by the natural effect of their constitutions, are frequently renewed or drawn back to their first principles."[2] Christian commitments led the founders to create a constitutional order that strictly limits the power of the national government, separates the powers it does have among different branches, and provides checks and balances to prevent any one institution or person from becoming tyrannical. They believed in a higher law, often called natural law, and thought that natural rights were based upon this law. Governments should not violate these rights, and, in fact, they have the affirmative responsibility to protect them. These are important principles for which we should fight today.

Many readers of this book are likely people of faith, who are busy doing important things, such as worshipping their Creator, raising children, earning paychecks, and serving others. To them, politics may seem like a frustrating, tainted distraction. Yet we cannot ignore the public square. We must take time to follow the news, engage our fellow citizens, vote, and perhaps even run for office. Our goal in doing so should not be to return America to some lost golden age, but to preserve and protect the remarkable constitutional order bequeathed to us by America's founders, and to encourage the passage of laws that promote the common good.[3]

I trust this book has put to rest the myth that the founders desired to build a high and impregnable wall of separation between church and state. Believers and civic leaders alike are free to bring their faith into the public square. There are important prudential reasons for not favoring one denomination or religion over others, but from an originalist perspective, the Establishment Clause provides no bar to exempting religious minorities from general laws, including "so help me God" in the Pledge of Allegiance, or permitting a Lutheran preschool to participate in a state program that provides safe playground surfaces.

Like James Wilson, the great Baptist minister Isaac Backus believed that a "frequent recurrence to the first principles of government . . . [is] absolutely necessary to preserve the great blessings of government and liberty."[4] In addition, he emphasized the necessity of firmly adhering "to justice, moderation, temperance, industry, and frugality."[5] One might expect a clergyman to emphasize the importance of morality, but as discussed in chapter 2, the founders universally agreed that virtue was necessary for republican government. As we engage in politics, we do well to keep the founders' syllogism in mind. At a minimum, this includes treating one's opponents with dignity, telling the truth, and engaging in political debate with civility.

A central theme in this book is that America's founders embraced a robust understanding of religious liberty. This important freedom, which many founders referred to as "sacred," is under increasing assault today.[6] If we are to be faithful to the founders' vision, we must insist that religious liberty be protected whenever possible. There are times when the state has a compelling interest in keeping someone from acting on his or her religious conviction (prohibiting human sacrifice is an obvious example), but these instances are few and far between. And Christians must insist that the religious liberty of non-Christian citizens be respected. Doing so is not only strategic, it is the right thing to do.

Concerns for religious liberty should inform our voting decisions, and readers might also consider supporting one of the many fine Christian organizations that fight for religious liberty in our nation's courtrooms every day. I am particularly grateful to the Christian Legal Society, whose former executive director, Samuel Ericsson, gave me an opportunity to serve as an intern in high school and then as a college student. He helped spark in me an interest in religious liberty and church-state relations that has been an important part of my professional career. Christian Legal Society continues to do excellent work under the leadership of David Nammo and Kim Colby. More recently, I have had the opportunity to work with the Alliance Defending Freedom, the Becket Fund for Religious Liberty, and the First Liberty Institute. All of these religious liberty advocacy organizations are more than worthy of our financial support.[7]

Having argued throughout this book that America did, in fact, have a Christian founding, I want to close by reemphasizing that the constitutional order the founders created has benefited citizens of every faith—as well as those who do not hold to any faith at all. One need not be a Christian to profit from limited government, checks and balances, and the rule of law. With respect to religion, the founders were clear that citizens of any faith are free to worship and act according to the dictates of their consciences. If we desire to honor their memory and legacy, we must continue to advocate these ideals today.

SUGGESTIONS FOR FURTHER READING

Dreisbach, Daniel L., and Mark David Hall, eds. *The Sacred Rights of Conscience: Selected Readings on Religious Liberty and Church-State Relations in the American Founding.* Indianapolis: Liberty Fund Press, 2009. A huge, thorough, and inexpensive collection of primary source documents on religious liberty and church-state relations in America from the early colonies to the early republic.

Dreisbach, Daniel L., and Mark David Hall, eds. *Great Christian Jurists in American History.* New York: Cambridge University Press, 2019. Profiles nineteen of America's greatest Christian jurists from the early colonial era to the present day.

Witte, John Jr., and Joel A. Nichols, eds. *Religion and the American Constitutional Experiment,* 4th ed. New York: Oxford University Press, 2016. An excellent, interdisciplinary overview of religious liberty in America from the early colonies to the present.

ACKNOWLEDGMENTS

In 2010, at the invitation of Matthew Spalding, I delivered a lecture at the Heritage Foundation in Washington, DC, entitled "Did America Have a Christian Founding?" We were pleasantly surprised when C-SPAN showed up to cover it, and later, when we learned that the published version of the talk had been downloaded more than three hundred thousand times. I am profoundly grateful to the foundation for the invitation to give the talk, and for their permission to use portions of the essay in this book.

It was at this lecture that I first met David Azzerad, now director of the B. Kenneth Simon Center for Principles and Politics at the Heritage Foundation. David and Arthur Milikh, the associate director and research fellow of the center, worked closely with me on a report entitled "Religious Accommodations and the Common Good," which is also available from the foundation. I am grateful for their partnership and look forward to working with them in the future.

"Religious Accommodations and the Common Good" was originally an expert opinion requested by the Alliance Defending Freedom for use in *State of Washington v. Arlene's Flowers* (2017). Playing a small role in that case gave me a greater appreciation for the hard work of the thousands of attorneys who fight regularly in our nation's courtrooms to protect what many founders called "the sacred rights of conscience."

I have also been encouraged by Barronelle Stutzman, Jack Phillips, and other business owners who are committed to bringing their religious and moral convictions into the marketplace.

An earlier version of the first chapter was published in *The Wiley Blackwell Companion to Religion and Politics in the U.S.*, ed. Barbara A. McGraw (West Sussex: Wiley Blackwell Publishing, 2016), 51–63. I am thankful to the press for permission to publish a revised version of the essay here.

Daniel L. Dreisbach, professor of justice, law, and criminology at American University, has been my most frequent collaborator over the years. We have edited five books together and have often discussed the problems addressed in this book. He was kind enough to read the entire manuscript, and it is far richer because of his comments.

I am also grateful to Herb Grey, Kevin R. C. Gutzman, Matthew J. Franck, Lydia Hall, and my research assistant, Kate Cvancara, for reading and making comments on this book's manuscript. My wife, Miriam, has read few of my scholarly works, but she was kind enough to read this book. I am thankful for her observations.

I have written, edited, or coedited a dozen academic books, but never one intended for the reading public. I am grateful to Giles Anderson of Anderson Literary Agency for helping secure a contract for *Did America Have a Christian Founding?*, and for his invaluable advice as I wrote the book. Webster Younce, Sujin Hong, Lori Lynch, and Stephanie Tresner at Nelson Books provided critical feedback and guidance for which I am most thankful. Of course, any errors or omissions are my responsibility.

I have taught at George Fox University since 2001 and plan to continue teaching as long as possible. I appreciate the excellent students and colleagues who make this such a wonderful place to work. I have particularly enjoyed teaching politics and in the William Penn Honors Program, one of the best great books courses of study in the nation. If you are a high school student and are interested in politics and/or great books, please give me a call—I would love to talk to you about either program. My contact information may be found at the George Fox University website: https://www.georgefox.edu/academics/undergrad /departments/polisci/hall.html.

George Fox University has proven to be a great place to balance teaching, service, and scholarship. I am grateful for the leadership of President Robin Baker, Provost Linda Samek, Associate Provost Laura Hartley, William Penn Honors Program Director Abigail Favale, and department chairs Paul Otto and Ron Mock. The university provided a much needed sabbatical that enabled me to complete this work in a timely fashion.

I am especially thankful for my wonderful wife and children, Miriam, Joshua, Lydia, and Anna, all of whom have long encouraged me to write a book that people will actually read. I pray that this is such a book.

NOTES

Introduction

1. Geoffrey R. Stone, "The World of the Framers: A Christian Nation?" *University of California Law Review* 56 (October 2008): 7–8.
2. Frank Lambert, *The Founding Fathers and the Place of Religion in America* (Princeton: Princeton University Press, 2003), 161.
3. Richard T. Hughes, *Myths America Lives By* (Urbana: University of Illinois Press, 2003), 50.
4. See also Charles A. Beard and Mary R. Beard, *The Rise of American Civilization* (New York: The Macmillan Company, 1930), 449; Edwin Gaustad, ed., *A Documentary History of Religion in America*, 2nd ed. (Grand Rapids: William B. Eerdmans, 1993), 1:227; Brooke Allen, *Moral Minority: Our Skeptical Founding Fathers* (Chicago: Ivan R. Dee, 2006), xiii; Ed Asner and Ed. Weinberger, *The Grouchy Historian: An Old-Time Lefty Defends Our Constitution Against Right-Wing Hypocrites and Nutjobs* (New York: Simon & Schuster, 2017), 4, 19; Matthew Stewart, *Nature's God: The Heretical Origins of the American Republic* (New York: W. W. Norton, 2014), 6; Harvey Kaye, *Thomas Paine and the Promise of America* (New York: Hill and Wang, 2005), 108; Frederic Smoler, "The Radical Revolution: An Interview with Gordon Wood," *American Heritage Magazine* 42

(December 1992), http://www.americanheritage.com/print/57789; Darryl G. Hart, *A Secular Faith: Why Christianity Favors the Separation of Church and State* (Chicago: Ivan R. Dee: 2006), 73; Steven K. Green, *The Second Disestablishment: Church and State in Nineteenth-Century America* (New York: Oxford University Press, 2010), 87; and William Martin, *With God on Our Side: The Rise of the Religious Right in America* (New York: Broadway, 1996), 376.

All the books and articles I criticize are by scholars or popular authors and are published by mainstream presses or journals. I could list many more, and more egregious examples of false or misleading claims if I referenced self-published polemical books, such as Chris Rodda, *Liars for Jesus: The Religious Right's Alternative Version of American History* (self-pub., 2006), and internet posts by nonexperts and/or overly enthusiastic activists.

5. This question is sometimes formulated in different ways. See, for example, John Fea, *Was America Founded as a Christian Nation?* (Louisville: Westminster John Knox, 2011); Daryl C. Cornett, ed., *Christian America? Perspective on Our Religious Heritage* (Nashville: B&H, 2011); John Wilsey, *One Nation Under God? An Evangelical Critique of Christian America* (Eugene: Pickwick, 2011); Mark A. Noll, Nathan O. Hatch, and George M. Marsden, *The Search for Christian America* (Westchester: Crossway, 1983); Jon Butler, "Why Revolutionary America Wasn't a 'Christian Nation,'" in *Religion and the New Republic*, ed. James H. Hutson (Lanham: Rowman & Littlefield, 2000), 91; and Mark David Hall, "Did America Have a Christian Founding?" The Heritage Foundation, June 7, 2011, https://www.heritage.org/political-process/report/did-america -have-christian-founding.

6. Technically, he was quoted as saying, "History is more or less bunk. It's tradition. We don't want tradition. We want to live in the present, and the only history that is worth a tinker's damn is the history that we make today." *Chicago Tribune*, May 25, 1916.

7. *Collected Works of James Wilson*, ed. Kermit L. Hall and Mark David Hall (Indianapolis: Liberty Fund Press, 2007), 1:698.

8. I include female founders not to be politically correct, but because I believe that individuals such as Abigail Adams and Mercy Otis Warren contributed significantly to the nation's founding. See, for instance, the essays on these fascinating women in Daniel L. Dreisbach, Mark David Hall, and Jeffry

Morrison, eds., *The Forgotten Founders on Religion and Public Life* (Notre Dame: University of Notre Dame Press, 2009).

I agree with Dreisbach that we should construe the term *founder* broadly to include "Americans from many walks of life who in the last half of the eighteenth century and early nineteenth century articulated the rights of colonists, secured independence from Great Britain, and established the new constitutional republic and its political institutions." Like Dreisbach, I agree that founders were not always on the winning side of every debate. So, for instance, we both consider Anti-Federalists such as George Mason and Patrick Henry to be founders. Dreisbach, "Famous Founders and Forgotten Founders: What's the Difference, and Does the Difference Matter?" in Gary L. Gregg and Mark David Hall, eds., *America's Forgotten Founders*, 2nd ed. (Wilmington: ISI, 2012), 3.

9. Advocates of "original intent" focus on the intent of the drafters of a text, whereas proponents of "original understanding" emphasize how the text was understood by citizens who debated and approved it (for instance, delegates to the state conventions that ratified the Constitution). America's founders disagreed on some important issues, but with respect to religious liberty and church-state relations there was a great deal of consensus.

10. *Everson v. Board of Education*, 330 U.S. 1 (1947), 33. Rutledge was dissenting from the Court's decision, but both the majority and dissenting opinions agreed that the First Amendment must be understood in light of the founders' views.

11. Mark David Hall, "Jeffersonian Walls and Madisonian Lines: The Supreme Court's Use of History in Religion Clause Cases," *High Court Quarterly Review* 5 (2009): 109–53. This is a slightly revised version of the article originally published in *Oregon Law Review* 85 (2006): 563–614.

12. See, for instance, President George W. Bush as quoted in "Lott Remarks on Segregation 'Wrong and Offensive,'" *The Irish Times*, December 13, 2002, https://web.archive.org/web/20150921020713/http://www.irishtimes.com /news/lott-remarks-on-segregation-wrong-and-offensive-1.1107399. See also Barack Obama's farewell speech, transcript available at the *Los Angeles Times*, January 10, 2017, http://www.latimes.com/politics/la-pol-obama-farewell -speech-transcript-20170110-story.html.

13. Religious Freedom Day is celebrated on January 16 of each year in commemoration of the Virginia General Assembly's passage of the Statute

for Religious Freedom on January 16, 1786. For more information and a collection of presidential proclamations honoring the day, see religiousfreedomday.com.

14. Barack Obama, "Presidential Proclamation—National Religious Freedom Day," January 15, 2015, White House, Washington, DC, https://obamawhitehouse.archives.gov/the-press-office/2015/01/15/presidential-proclamation-religious-freedom-day-2015.

15. *Burwell v. Hobby Lobby Stores*, 573 U.S. ___ (2014).

16. *Hosanna-Tabor Evangelical Lutheran Church & School v. Equal Employment Opportunity Commission*, 132 S. Ct. 694 (2012), 710.

17. David G. Dalin, "Jews, Judaism, and the American Founding," in *Faith and the Founders of the American Republic*, ed. Daniel L. Dreisbach and Mark David Hall (New York: Oxford University Press, 2014), 63. Of course, definitive records demonstrating everyone *did* identify himself or herself as a Protestant, Catholic, or Jew simply don't exist. But my claim is more than plausible given the data we do have, and the lack of evidence indicating that there were more than a handful of non-Christians or atheists. Like virtually all scholars who study this topic, by "colonists" I mean immigrants of European descent.

18. Barry A. Kosmin and Seymour P. Lachman, *One Nation Under God: Religion in Contemporary American Society* (New York: Harmony, 1993), 28–29.

19. By "orthodox" I mean that they adhered to fundamental Christian doctrines as articulated in the Apostles' or Nicene Creeds.

20. For instance, Butler, "Why Revolutionary America Wasn't a 'Christian Nation,'" 91.

21. See, for example, claims made by the prominent Christian historians Noll, Hatch, and Marsden in *Search for Christian America*, 53–54, 95–100. I address these issues in the sequel to this book.

22. Alan Gibson provides an overview of scholarly attempts to understand the intellectual influences on America's founders in *Interpreting the Founding: Guide to the Enduring Debates Over the Origins and Foundations of the American Republic* (Lawrence: University Press of Kansas, 2006). Like many scholars, he neglects the possibility that Christian ideas had an important influence in the era.

23. Of course, Christianity was not the *only* significant influence on America's founders, and it did not influence each founder in the exact same manner.

24. Gary DeMar, *America's Christian Heritage* (Nashville: B&H, 2003), 13.

25. John Winthrop, quoted in Daniel L. Dreisbach and Mark David Hall, eds., *The Sacred Rights of Conscience: Selected Readings on Religious Liberty and Church-State Relations in the American Founding* (Indianapolis: Liberty Fund Press, 2009), 131.

26. Excellent books that make these points include David D. Hall, *A Reforming People: Puritanism and the Transformation of Public Life in New England* (New York: Alfred A. Knopf, 2011), and Michael P. Winship, *Godly Republicanism: Puritans, Pilgrims, and a City on a Hill* (Cambridge: Harvard University Press, 2012).

27. Dreisbach and Hall, *Sacred Rights of Conscience*, 93. Upon occasion, I modernize spelling and punctuation in quotations when doing so makes them easier to read without changing their meaning.

28. Dreisbach and Hall, *Sacred Rights of Conscience*, 94.

29. Fea, *Was America Founded as a Christian Nation?*, 82.

30. Dreisbach and Hall, *Sacred Rights of Conscience*, 84.

31. Dreisbach and Hall, *Sacred Rights of Conscience*, 84.

32. Dreisbach and Hall, *Sacred Rights of Conscience*, 116–19.

33. Dreisbach and Hall, *Sacred Rights of Conscience*, 118. Rhode Island, Pennsylvania, Delaware, and New Jersey did not have established churches. New York had establishments in select counties. Most colonies had religious tests for office, and all had laws encouraging and protecting Christianity and Christian morality.

34. Even though I disagree with specific claims made by some authors, I do not mean to suggest that there is nothing of value in their works. For instance, I have read virtually every book written by Mark Noll, George Marsden, and Nathan Hatch and have benefited tremendously from them. Yet a few of the books I critique, such as Stewart's *Nature's God*, are uniformly bad.

35. That is, among Americans of European descent. Accurate statistics are difficult to come by for African Americans and Native Americans.

36. Dreisbach and Hall, *Sacred Rights of Conscience*, 464.

37. Peter A. Lillback and Jerry Newcombe, *George Washington's Sacred Fire* (Bryn Mawr: Providence Forum Press, 2006), 321–22. See also Daniel L. Dreisbach, *Reading the Bible with the Founding Fathers* (New York: Oxford University Press, 2017), 318, for scriptural references in the same letter and for examples of prominent scholars who assert that Washington "rarely alluded to or quoted the Scriptures."

38. Lillback and Newcombe, *Sacred Fire*, 211–27.

Chapter 1: The Myth of the Founders' Deism

1. An earlier version of this essay was published as "Were Any of the Founders Deists?" in *The Wiley Blackwell Companion to Religion and Politics in the U.S.*, ed. Barbara A. McGraw (West Sussex: Wiley Blackwell, 2016), 51–63. It is used here by the kind permission of the publisher. Historian Darren Staloff makes an argument similar to mine in "Deism and the Founders," but we arrived at our conclusions independently of each other. His essay is available in Daniel L. Dreisbach and Mark David Hall, eds., *Faith and the Founders of the American Republic* (New York: Oxford University Press, 2014), 13–33.

    I use *myth* here and elsewhere in its popular sense of being "an unfounded or false notion," as defined in Merriam-Webster's online dictionary, https://www.merriam-webster.com/dictionary/myth (accessed December 1, 2018).

2. Frederic Smoler, "The Radical Revolution: An Interview with Gordon Wood," *American Heritage Magazine* 42 (December 1992), http://www .americanheritage.com/print/57789; Edwin Gaustad, ed., *A Documentary History of Religion in America*, 2nd ed. (Grand Rapids: William B. Eerdmans, 1993), 1:227; Brooke Allen, *Moral Minority: Our Skeptical Founding Fathers* (Chicago: Ivan R. Dee, 2006), xiii; Mark A. Noll, Nathan O. Hatch, and George M. Marsden, *The Search for Christian America* (Westchester: Crossway, 1983), 73–74; and Matthew Stewart, *Nature's God: The Heretical Origins of the American Republic* (New York: W. W. Norton, 2014), 6.

    See also R. Laurence Moore and Isaac Kramnick, *Godless Citizens in a Godly Republic: Atheists in American Public Life* (New York: W. W. Norton, 2018), xiii ("Many of the prominent white men who wrote the nation's fundamental documents called themselves deists. They believed in a designer Creator, but in none of the core beliefs of Christianity"); Garry Wills, *Head and Heart: A History of Christianity in America* (New York: Penguin Books, 2007), 153 ("The reaction to the Great Awakening provided an American Unitarian boost that made Deism the religion of the educated class by the middle of the eighteenth century. Legal scholar William Lee Miller writes that the chief founders of the nation were all Deists—he lists Washington, Franklin, Adams, Jefferson, Madison, Hamilton, and Paine, though many more leaders of the founding era could be added"); Richard

T. Hughes, *Myths America Lives By* (Urbana: University of Illinois Press, 2003), 50 ("Most of the American Founders embraced some form of Deism, not historically orthodox Christianity"); Harvey Kaye, *Thomas Paine and the Promise of America* (New York: Hill and Wang, 2005), 108 ("Many of the nation's original Founders subscribed to some version of religious rationalism"); Darryl G. Hart, *A Secular Faith: Why Christianity Favors the Separation of Church and State* (Chicago: Ivan R. Dee: 2006), 73 ("Most of the so-called Founding Fathers, from Jefferson and Adams to George Washington, Benjamin Franklin, and James Madison were generally indifferent to most of the claims of the denominations, from the vicarious atonement to the real presence of Christ in the Lord's Supper"); Steven K. Green, *The Second Disestablishment: Church and State in Nineteenth-Century America* (New York: Oxford University Press, 2010), 87 ("Although many of the nation's elites privately embraced deism, *The Age of Reason* and other works popularized irreligion among the laboring and working classes"); Steven J. Keillor, *This Rebellious House: American History & the Truth of Christianity* (Downers Grove: InterVarsity, 1996), 85 ("Many of America's 'Founding Fathers' were not Christians in any orthodox sense"); Richard Dawkins, *The God Delusion* (Boston: Houghton Mifflin, 2006), 38–39 ("No doubt many of [the founders were deists], although it has been argued that the greatest of them might have been atheists"); C. Gregg Singer, *A Theological Interpretation of American History*, rev. ed. (Philadelphia: Presbyterian and Reformed Publishing Co., 1981), 24 ("Deism . . . provided that political philosophy which would produce the American Revolution"); Bill Press, *How the Republicans Stole Christmas: The Republican Party's Declared Monopoly on Religion and What Democrats Can Do to Take It Back* (New York: Doubleday, 2005), 43 ("[The Founders] did believe in God, but most of them only in the Enlightenment or deist sense of God as 'watchmaker'—a Supreme Being who created us, then wound us up and let us run on our own"); and Charles A. Beard and Mary R. Beard, *The Rise of American Civilization* (New York: Macmillan, 1930), 449 ("When the crisis came, Jefferson, Paine, John Adams, Washington, Franklin, Madison, and many lesser lights were to be reckoned among either Unitarians or Deists. It was not Cotton Mather's God to whom the authors of the Declaration of Independence appealed; it was to 'Nature's God'").

3. Alan Wolfe, "Keeping the Faith at Arm's Length," review of *The Faiths of the Founding Fathers* by David L. Holmes, *Realistic Visionary* by Peter R.

Henriques, and *American Gospel* by Jon Meacham, *New York Times*, May 7, 2006, Sunday Book Review, http://www.nytimes.com/2006/05/07/books /review/07wolfe.html. There is no single definition of deism, but the one offered above is widely used. Compare with Christopher Grasso, *Skepticism and American Faith: From the Revolution to the Civil War* (New York: Oxford University Press, 2018), 26 ("'Deism' is usually associated with belief in a noninterventionist Creator, reliance upon what reason can discern in the natural world, and skepticism about miracles, mysticism, the divine inspiration of the scriptures, and the divinity of Christ").

4. I do not discuss clergy in this chapter, even though I believe they played an important role in the American founding. There is evidence that ministers such as Ebenezer Gay, Charles Chauncy, Jonathan Mayhew, and Elihu Palmer embraced deism or something akin to it. However, Mark A. Noll argues there is little reason to doubt that the vast majority of clerics in the era were anything other than orthodox Christians. Noll, *America's God: From Jonathan Edwards to Abraham Lincoln* (New York: Oxford University Press, 2005), 138–45.

5. *The Papers of Benjamin Franklin*, ed. Leonard W. Labaree (New Haven: Yale University Press, 1959), 1:57–71; and *Benjamin Franklin's Autobiography*, ed. J. A. Leo Lemay and P. M. Zall (New York: W. W. Norton, 1986), 46.

6. *Papers of Benjamin Franklin*, 1:57–60.

7. *Benjamin Franklin's Autobiography*, 45–46.

8. Daniel L. Dreisbach and Mark David Hall, eds., *The Sacred Rights of Conscience: Selected Readings on Religious Liberty and Church-State Relations in the American Founding* (Indianapolis: Liberty Fund Press, 2009), 348–49.

9. "Franklin to Stiles, March 9, 1790," in *Benjamin Franklin: Writings*, ed. J. A. Leo LeMay (New York: Library of America, 1987), 178–80.

10. Susan Jacoby, *Freethinkers: A History of American Secularism* (New York: Metropolitan, 2004), 18. See also Kerry S. Walters, *Rational Infidels: The American Deists* (Durango: Longwood Academic, 1992), xiii, 8, 92; and Kerry S. Walters, *The American Deists: Voices of Reason and Dissent in the Early Republic* (Lawrence: University Press of Kansas, 1992), 51–105.

11. Part one of *The Age of Reason* was published in 1794, part two in 1795, and an obscure and little-known part three in 1807. According to Gary Nash, seventeen American editions of *The Age of Reason* appeared from 1794 to

1796. Gary Nash, "The American Clergy and the French Revolution," *The William and Mary Quarterly*, 3rd series (July 1965): 402.

12. *The Works of John Adams*, ed. Charles Francis Adams (Boston: Charles C. Little and James Brown, 1850), 3:421, 9:73; and "Samuel Adams to Thomas Paine, November 30, 1802," in *Paine: Collected Writings*, ed. Eric Foner (New York: Library of America, 1995), 415.

13. "Rush to John Dickinson, February 16, 1796," in *Letters of Benjamin Rush*, ed. L. H. Butterfield (Princeton: Princeton University Press, 1951), 2:770; Charles Carroll, quoted in Bradley J. Birzer, *American Cicero: The Life of Charles Carroll* (Wilmington: ISI, 2010), 188; and Zephaniah Swift, *A System of Laws of the State of Connecticut* (Windham: John Byrne, 1796), 2:323–24.

14. David J. Volker, "Thomas Paine's Civil Religion of Reason," in Daniel L. Dreisbach, Mark David Hall, and Jeffry Morrison, eds., *The Forgotten Founders on Religion and Public Life* (Notre Dame: University of Notre Dame Press, 2009), 172, 187–88; William Paterson, Fourth of July Oration, 1798, Princeton University Library, Paterson Collection, Box 1, Folder 14; and "John Jay to Uzal Ogden, February 14, 1796" in *The Life of John Jay*, ed. William Jay (New York: J. & J. Harper, 1833), 2:266.

15. Ian Shapiro, "Introduction: Thomas Paine, America's First Public Intellectual," in *Selected Writings of Thomas Paine*, ed. Ian Shapiro and Jane E. Calvert (New Haven: Yale University Press, 2014), xii.

16. Adrienne Koch and William Peden, eds., *The Life and Selected Writings of Thomas Jefferson* (1944; repr., New York: Random House, 1993), 634. A good overview of Jefferson's faith may be found in Edwin S. Gaustad, *Sworn on the Altar of God: A Religious Biography of Thomas Jefferson* (Grand Rapids: Eerdmans, 1996).

17. Dreisbach and Hall, *Sacred Rights of Conscience*, 290–92, 482–86. Jefferson's *Notes on the State of Virginia* was initially published anonymously, and he may not have intended to have them published at all. Gene Zechmeister, introduction to *Notes on the State of Virginia*, December 20, 2013, https://www.monticello.org/site/research-and-collections/notes-state-virginia.

18. "Adams to Jefferson, November 4, 1816," in *Adams-Jefferson Letters*, ed. Lester J. Cappon (Chapel Hill: University of North Carolina Press), 2:494.

19. "John Adams to John Quincy Adams, March 28, 1816," in James H. Hutson,

The Founders on Religion: A Book of Quotations (Princeton: Princeton University Press, 2005), 121.

20. Dreisbach and Hall, *Sacred Rights of Conscience*, 519.

21. David L. Holmes, *The Faiths of the Founding Fathers* (New York: Oxford University Press, 2006), 47, 65.

22. John Fea, *Was America Founded as a Christian Nation?* (Louisville: Westminster John Knox, 2011), 185.

23. *The Papers of George Washington: Presidential Series*, ed. Dorothy Twohig et al. (Charlottesville: University of Virginia Press, 1999), 8:33.

24. It is unlikely that Washington had an extramarital affair, but reports that he did surface periodically. See John L. Smith Jr., "The Alleged Amorous Affairs of Washington," *Journal of the American Revolution* (March 10, 2016), https://allthingsliberty.com/2016/03/the-alleged-amorous-affairs-of-washington/.

25. Bishop [William] Meade, *Old Churches, Ministers, and Families of Virginia* (Philadelphia: J. B. Lippencott, 1857), 2:99–101.

26. John Marshall, *The Life of George Washington* (Philadelphia: James Crissy, 1832), 2:445.

27. Quoted in Gilbert Chinard, ed., *George Washington as the French Knew Him: A Collection of Texts* (Princeton: Princeton University Press, 1940), 119.

28. Joseph Ellis, *His Excellency: George Washington* (New York: Vintage Books, 2004), 45.

29. Daniel L. Dreisbach, "Famous Founders and Forgotten Founders: What's the Difference, and Does the Difference Matter?" in Gary L. Gregg and Mark David Hall, eds., *America's Forgotten Founders*, 2nd ed. (Wilmington: ISI, 2012), 22.

30. Tim LaHaye, *Faith of Our Founding Fathers* (Brentwood: Wolgemuth & Hyatt, 1987), 113.

31. See, for instance, Allen's *Moral Minority*, where she asserts that Wythe, Morris, and Livingston were deists or otherwise heterodox, but that Rush was a "devout Christian" (29, 158, 160, 102). Holmes, in *Faiths of the Founding Fathers*, devotes an entire chapter asserting that Monroe was an "Episcopalian of Deistic tendencies," yet cites no instance of him rejecting any tenet of orthodox Christianity or embracing deism (99–107).

32. Of course, it is impossible to prove that Allen never spoke of God's intervention in human affairs. I can only say that I have found no record of him doing so. In *Reason: The Only Oracle of Man*, he denied the possibility of

miracles; see especially chapter 6, section 4: "Prayer Cannot Be Attended with Miraculous Consequences."

33. Peter A. Lillback and Jerry Newcombe, *George Washington's Sacred Fire* (Bryn Mawr: Providence Forum Press, 2006), 576.

34. "Washington to John Augustine Washington, July 18, 1755," in *The Papers of George Washington: Colonial Series*, ed. W. W. Abbot et al. (Charlottesville: University Press of Virginia, 1983), 1:343.

35. Hutson, *Founders on Religion*, 176.

36. Dreisbach and Hall, *Sacred Rights of Conscience*, 452. See also Hutson, *Founders on Religion*, 294.

37. Dreisbach and Hall, *Sacred Rights of Conscience*, 348–49.

38. See Mark David Hall, *Roger Sherman and the Creation of the American Republic* (New York: Oxford University Press, 2013).

39. Those who would deny the influence of Christianity in America's founding think it significant that the Convention did not act on Franklin's suggestion; see, for example, Isaac Kramnick and R. Laurence Moore, *The Godless Constitution: The Case Against Religious Correctness* (New York: W. W. Norton, 1996), 34. As I explain in my book on Roger Sherman, it is most likely that they rejected the proposal because, in Hamilton's words, to bring in clergy "might at this late day, 1. bring on it some disagreeable animadversions. & 2. lead the public to believe that the embarrassments and dissentions within the convention, had suggested this measure" (Hall, *Roger Sherman*, 108–9).

40. Dreisbach and Hall, *Sacred Rights of Conscience*, 350.

41. Kramnick and Moore, *Godless Constitution*, 31. It is true that there are not many references to God in *The Federalist Papers*, but as I argue in the next chapter, the influence of Christian ideas cannot be measured simply by counting references to the Deity.

     An online and searchable version of *The Federalist Papers* is available at http://oll.libertyfund.org/titles/carey-the-federalist-gideon-ed (accessed September 7, 2018). Liberty Fund's Online Library of Liberty is an excellent website for primary source documents from the American founding (among other things).

42. "Alexander Hamilton to an unknown recipient, April 13, 1804," in *Papers of Alexander Hamilton*, ed. Harold Syrett et al. (New York: Columbia University Press, 1979), 27:219.

43. Thomas Paine, *The American Crisis* (March 21, 1778); and *Paine: Collected Writings*, 166.

44. Dreisbach and Hall, *Sacred Rights of Conscience*, 220.

45. For instance, Holmes, *Faiths of the Founding Fathers*, 47, 65; Fea, *Was America Founded as a Christian Nation?*, 131–33, 136; Frank Lambert, *The Founding Fathers and the Place of Religion in America* (Princeton: Princeton University Press, 2003), 167; and Jon Butler, *Awash in a Sea of Faith: Christianizing the American People* (Cambridge: Harvard University Press, 1990), 196.

46. Westminster Standards, 1:10; 5:1, 2, 6; 19:5; 23:1; 1:1, 7; 5; 21:5; *The Works of the Late Reverend and Learned Isaac Watts* (London, 1753), 4:356; see also *The Windham Herald*, April 15, 1797, 4.

47. *Works of the Late Reverend and Learned Isaac Watts*, 4:356.

48. Jeffry H. Morrison, "Political Theology in the Declaration of Independence," a paper delivered at a conference on the Declaration of Independence, Princeton University, April 5–6, 2002.

49. "Jefferson to Henry Lee, May 8, 1825," in Koch and Peden, *Life and Selected Writings of Thomas Jefferson*, 656–57.

50. *Theistic rationalism* is a phrase coined by Gregg Frazer, and it is more accurate than deism as applied to a handful of America's founders. Frazer is careful to limit his claims to "key" founders, but even so, he overstates the attraction of this belief system in the founding era. Gregg L. Frazer, *The Religious Beliefs of America's Founders: Reason, Revelation, and Revolution* (Lawrence: University Press of Kansas, 2012). My review of Frazer's book may be found in the *Journal of American History* 99 (March 2013): 1226–27.

51. Hamilton immigrated to America in 1773 when he was about eighteen years old (his exact birthday is disputed); Jefferson was in France from 1785 to 1789; and Adams was in Europe from 1778 to 1788.

52. Sydney E. Ahlstrom, *A Religious History of the American People* (Garden City: Doubleday, 1975), 1:426.

53. Harry S. Stout, "Preaching the Insurrection," *Christian History* 15 (1996): 17.

54. According to Charles O. Paullin, 56 percent of churches in America in 1776 were in the Reformed tradition. Paullin, *Atlas of the Historical Geography of the United States* (Washington, DC: Carnegie Institution, 1932), 50. Edwin Gaustad and Philip Barlow found that 63 percent of the churches in 1780 were Calvinist. Gaustad and Barlow, *New Historical Atlas of Religion in America* (New York: Oxford University Press, 2001), 8. The two estimates

for 1776—56 percent (Paullin) and 75 percent (Ahlstrom)—are not necessarily in conflict if Reformed churches had larger congregations than non-Reformed churches.

55. I have not explored all of these founders in depth, but I did look into each of them when I wrote *Roger Sherman*. That book focuses on Sherman, but I use him as a lens to shine light on the contributions a wide range of Reformed founders made in the era.

56. Hughes, *Myths America Lives By*, 50.

57. Lambert, *Founding Fathers*, 176, quoting and applying to Americans a deistic conception of God offered by J. C. D. Clark in *English Society, 1688–1832: Ideology, Social Structure and Political Practice during the Ancien Regime* (Cambridge: Cambridge University Press, 1985), 279–80.

Chapter 2: The United States Does Not Have a Godless Constitution

1. Isaac Kramnick and R. Laurence Moore, *The Godless Constitution: The Case Against Religious Correctness* (New York: W. W. Norton, 1996), 27; Richard T. Hughes, *Myths America Lives By* (Urbana: University of Illinois Press, 2003), 67; Susan Jacoby, *Freethinkers: A History of American Secularism* (New York: Metropolitan, 2004), 28; Derek Davis, *Religion and the Continental Congress, 1774–1789* (New York: Oxford University Press, 2000), 205; and Joseph J. Ellis, *American Creation: Triumphs and Tragedies at the Founding of the Republic* (New York: Alfred A. Knopf, 2007), 8.

See also Steven J. Keillor, *This Rebellious House: American History & the Truth of Christianity* (Downers Grove: InterVarsity, 1996), 96–97 ("A 'remarkably secular' Convention produced 'a perfectly secular text.' . . . Compared to state constitutions, it was irreligious: it was a product of the irreligious Enlightenment"); Robert Boston, *Why the Religious Right Is Wrong About Separation of Church and State*, 2nd ed. (Amherst: Prometheus, 2003), 6 ("The Constitution fashioned in 1787, largely the work of Madison, is a secular document"); William Martin, *With God on Our Side: The Rise of the Religious Right in America* (New York: Broadway, 1996), 375 ("In keeping with their determination to separate religion and government, the framers wrote a constitution that was entirely secular"); Brooke Allen, *Moral Minority: Our Skeptical Founding Fathers* (Chicago: Ivan R. Dee, 2006), xiv ("The United States of America was a purely secular project. The absence of God in the new nation's Constitution was a highly deliberate, indeed a vital part of that project"); Bill Press, *How the Republicans Stole Christmas: The Republican Party's Declared Monopoly on Religion and What Democrats Can Do to Take It Back* (New York: Doubleday, 2005), 51 ("The farsighted Americans who gathered in Philadelphia . . . founded the nation on a secular document"); Frank Lambert, *The Founding Fathers and the Place of Religion in America* (Princeton: Princeton University Press, 2003), 238 ("The creation of a secular state resulted from the enlightened conviction of many leading Founders who thought that, by natural right, church and state ought to be separate"); Jon Butler, *Awash in a Sea of Faith: Christianizing the American People* (Cambridge: Harvard University Press, 1990), 214 ("Much of the postrevolutionary optimism was openly secular, not religious, and reflected the Founding Fathers' Enlightenment convictions"); Morton Borden, *Jews, Turks, and Infidels* (Chapel Hill: University of North Carolina Press, 1984), 10 ("Among the educated classes of America, the cult of reason was widespread"); and Brandon J. O'Brien, *Demanding Liberty: An Untold Story of American Religious Freedom* (Downers Grove: InterVarsity, 2018), 139 ("It is easy to identify 'founding fathers' of the Revolutionary period—signers of the Declaration of Independence, framers of the Constitution, early presidents— who were not men of faith and who were self-consciously committed to founding America on *secular* principles, not Christian ones" [emphasis original]).

2. Daniel L. Dreisbach and Mark David Hall, eds., *The Sacred Rights of Conscience: Selected Readings on Religious Liberty and Church-State Relations in the American Founding* (Indianapolis: Liberty Fund Press, 2009), 225.

3. Quoted in Dreisbach and Hall, *Sacred Rights of Conscience*, 245.

4. Max Farrand, ed., *The Records of the Federal Convention of 1787* (New Haven: Yale University Press, 1966), 2:663. Scholars and activists debate whether this line is part of Article VII, a line in the Constitution that follows Article VII, or an extraconstitutional line. Given my argument above, it is not necessary to engage in this controversy. For a good, detailed discussion of the issue, see Akhil Reed Amar, *America's Unwritten Constitution: The Precedents and Principles We Live By* (New York: Basic Books, 2012), 63–79.

5. Quoted in Daniel L. Dreisbach, ed., *Religion and Politics in the Early Republic: Jasper Adams and the Church-State Debate* (Lexington: University Press of Kentucky, 1996), 63.

6. B. F. Morris, *Christian Life and Character of the Civil Institutions of the*

United States, Developed in the Official and Historical Annals of the Republic (Philadelphia: George W. Childs, 1864), 262.

7. "Declaration of the Rights of Man—1789," Yale Law School, Avalon Project, http://avalon.law.yale.edu/18th_century/rightsof.asp (accessed March 18, 2018); and William Lee Miller, *The Business of Next May: James Madison and the Founding* (Charlottesville: University of Virginia Press, 1992), 113.

8. For further discussion, see Daniel L. Dreisbach, "In Search of a Christian Commonwealth: An Examination of Selected Nineteenth-Century Commentaries on References to God and the Christian Religion in the Constitution," *Baylor Law Review* 48 (1996): 928–1000.

9. Even writers such as Edward Gibbon, who was highly critical of Christianity, continued to use the convention. See, for instance, Gibbon, *The History of the Decline and Fall of the Roman Empire* (London: Straham and Cadell, 1776), 1:1.

10. Richard R. John, "Taking Sabbatarianism Seriously: The Postal System, the Sabbath, and the Transformation of American Political Culture," *Journal of the Early Republic* 4 (Winter 1990): 528.

11. See Gordon Lloyd, "Day-by-Day Summary of the Convention," http://teachingamericanhistory.org/convention/summary/ (accessed November 20, 2018); and Farrand, *Records of the Federal Convention of 1787*, vols. 1 and 2.

12. Quoted in Dreisbach and Hall, *Sacred Rights of Conscience*, 350.

13. See US House of Representatives, "List of All Weekend Sessions," https://history.house.gov/Institution/Saturday-Sunday/All/ (accessed November 20, 2018). I was unable to find a similarly comprehensive study for the US Senate, but for a partial study, see US Senate, "Sunday Sessions of the Senate (since 1861)," https://www.senate.gov/pagelayout/reference/five_column_table/Sunday_Sessions_of_the_Senate.htm (accessed November 28, 2018).

It is not my position that members of Congress never worked on Sunday, or that national legislators always respected the Sabbath. In 1810, Congress passed a statute requiring postmasters to open their offices and deliver mail on any day it arrived—including Sunday. This law led to a great deal of controversy between 1810 and 1830. Sunday mail delivery was eventually eliminated, although not until 1912. See John, "Taking Sabbatarianism Seriously," 517–67.

14. Dreisbach and Hall, *Sacred Rights of Conscience*, 349–50.

15. Dreisbach and Hall, *Sacred Rights of Conscience*, 388.

16. Dreisbach and Hall, *Sacred Rights of Conscience*, 397.

17. Daniel L. Dreisbach points out that Article III's requirement that "convictions for treason be supported by 'the testimony of two witnesses' conforms to a familiar biblical mandate for conviction and punishment (Deut. 17:6)." Dreisbach, *Reading the Bible with the Founding Fathers* (New York: Oxford University Press, 2017), 46–47.

18. Dreisbach and Hall, *Sacred Rights of Conscience*, 351–52.

19. One particularly concerned group was the Covenanters. This Presbyterian sect originated in Scotland, and by the Revolutionary era there were approximately five thousand Covenanters in America. By the mid-1830s, this number had grown to twenty thousand, and during the eighteenth and nineteenth centuries, they authored some of the leading critiques of America's "godless" constitution. They complained loudly, but it is important to remember that they were always a tiny percentage of America's population (roughly 0.2 percent in the Revolutionary era). An excellent overview of the Covenanters may be found in Joseph S. Moore, *Founding Sins: How a Group of Antislavery Radicals Fought to Put Christ into the Constitution* (New York: Oxford University Press, 2016), see page 164 for the number of Covenanters in America.

20. See Dreisbach and Hall, *Sacred Rights of Conscience*, 351–65.

21. Dreisbach and Hall, *Sacred Rights of Conscience*, 353.

22. Pauline Maier, *Ratification: The People Debate the Constitution, 1787–1788* (New York: Simon & Schuster, 2010). After the Constitution was ratified, James Madison convinced members of the First Federal Congress to debate and propose the amendments that we now know as the Bill of Rights.

23. For example, Allen, *Moral Minority*, xiv; and Frank Lambert, *Separation of Church and State: Founding Principle of Religious Liberty* (Macon: Mercer University Press, 2014), 117.

24. Matthew Stewart, *Nature's God: The Heretical Origins of the American Republic* (New York: W. W. Norton, 2014), 147–48.

25. Stewart, *Nature's God*, 3.

26. Stewart compiles praise for his book on his personal website, http://mwstewart.com/books/natures-god/ (accessed March 5, 2018). When I visited the website in spring 2018, he included three critical reviews under the heading: "Fatwas, Partisan Hack-Jobs, Evidence of Fear & Loathing Among Conservative 'Intellectuals,' etc." Among these "intellectuals" were James Hutson, PhD in history from Yale and chief of manuscripts at the Library of Congress, and Tracy Robert McKenzie, PhD in history from Vanderbilt and

chair of the history department at Wheaton College. Hutson and McKenzie are excellent, widely respected historians. Stewart's dismissal of them as partisan hacks helps demonstrate that he is far more interested in engaging in polemics than history. When I revisited his website on December 1, 2018, this section had been removed. I offer an extensive critique of Stewart's book in *Christian Scholar's Review* XLIV (Spring 2015): 285–91.

27. Many academics have argued about the religious convictions of these thinkers and whether their ideas are compatible with orthodox Christianity. These debates are interesting and important, but they are irrelevant for present purposes. My contention here is that, to the extent to which America's founders utilized these thinkers, they borrowed ideas or arguments that were compatible with orthodox Christianity, and, in fact, were often developed before the Enlightenment by indisputably Christian thinkers. For an example of how this argument plays out with respect to John Locke in America, see Mark David Hall, *Roger Sherman and the Creation of the American Republic* (New York: Oxford University Press, 2013), 12–40.

28. Carl Becker, *The Declaration of Independence* (New York: Vintage, 1922), 27.

29. Kramnick and Moore, *Godless Constitution*, 72; and Barbara A. McGraw, *Rediscovering America's Sacred Ground: Public Religion and Pursuit of the Good in a Pluralistic America* (Albany: SUNY Press, 2003), xv. See also, William Ebenstein and Alan Ebenstein, *Great Political Thinkers: Plato to the Present*, 6th ed. (New York: Thomas Wadsworth, 2000), 388 ("The main elements of the American constitutional system—limited government, inalienable individual rights, inviolability of property—are all directly traceable to Locke"); Isaac Kramnick, *Republicanism and Bourgeois Radicalism: Political Ideology in Late Eighteenth-Century England and America* (Ithaca: Cornell University Press, 1990), 293; and Geoffrey R. Stone, *Sex and the Constitution: Sex, Religion, and Law from America's Origins to the Twenty-First Century* (New York: W. W. Norton, 2017), 111.

30. John Dunn, "The Politics of Locke in England and America in the Eighteenth Century," in *John Locke: Problems and Perspectives: A Collection of New Essays*, ed. John Yolton (Cambridge: Cambridge University Press, 1969), 45–80, see esp. 69–71. Dunn concludes with respect to the American Revolution, "For the American population at large the revolution may have been about many things, but in a very few cases can it possibly have been thought to have been in any sense about the *Two Treatises of Government* of John Locke" (80).

31. John Locke, *An Essay Concerning the True Original Extent and End of Civil Government* (Boston, 1773), http://www.let.rug.nl/usa/documents /1651–1700/john-locke-essay-on-government/.

32. Donald S. Lutz, "The Relative Influence of European Writers on Late Eighteenth-Century American Political Thought," *American Political Science Review* 78 (1984): 189–97, esp. 192–93. See also James P. Byrd, *Sacred Scripture, Sacred War: The Bible and the American Revolution* (New York: Oxford University Press, 2013), 16 ("In Revolutionary America, Congregationalist ministers alone preached over 2,000 sermons each week. Sermons were published at four times the rate of political pamphlets and were more influential as well").

33. Joyce Appleby, "The American Heritage—The Heirs and the Disinherited," *Journal of American History* 74 (1987): 809.

34. Dreisbach, *Reading the Bible*. See also Carl J. Richard, *The Founders and the Bible* (Lanham: Rowman & Littlefield, 2016).

35. "Benjamin Franklin to Samuel Cooper, May 15, 1781," in *The Works of Benjamin Franklin*, ed. John Bigelow (New York: G. P. Putnam's Sons, 1904), 423–24.

36. James H. Hutson, *Religion and the Founding of the American Republic* (Washington, DC: Library of Congress, 1998), 81.

37. Dreisbach and Hall, *Sacred Rights of Conscience*, 611.

38. *Of the Mode of Education Proper in a Republic* (1798), in *The Selected Writings of Benjamin Rush*, ed. Dagobert D. Runes (New York: The Philosophical Library, 1947), 88.

39. "John Adams to Zabdiel Adams, June 21, 1776," quoted in James Hutson, *Forgotten Features of the Founding: The Recovery of Religious Themes in the Early American Republic* (Lanham: Lexington Books, 2003), 81.

40. "John Adams to Benjamin Rush, August 28, 1811," quoted in James H. Hutson, *The Founders on Religion: A Book of Quotations* (Princeton: Princeton University Press, 2005), 191.

41. Dreisbach and Hall, *Sacred Rights of Conscience*, 471.

42. Elizur Goodrich, "'The Principles of Civil Union and Happiness,' An Election Day Sermon Preached on May 10, 1787," in Ellis Sandoz, ed., *Political Sermons of the American Founding Era, 1735–1805*, 2nd ed. (Indianapolis: Liberty Fund Press, 1998), 1:918–19.

43. *Runkel v. Winemiller*, 4 H. & McH. 429, at 450 (1799). Chase's lower court

opinion was issued in 1796, but the Maryland Supreme Court decision in which his opinion was quoted was published in 1799.

44. Quoted in David Brion Davis, ed., *The Fear of Conspiracy: Images of Un-American Subversion from the Revolution to the Present* (Ithaca: Cornell University Press, 1971), 46.

45. Dreisbach and Hall, *Sacred Rights of Conscience*, xxvii.

46. Dreisbach and Hall, *Sacred Rights of Conscience*, 298.

47. Dreisbach, *Reading the Bible*, 97–104, 211–27.

48. John Fea, *Was America Founded as a Christian Nation?* (Louisville: Westminster John Knox, 2011), xxiv.

49. Fea, *Was America Founded as a Christian Nation?*, 180. Fea likewise suggests that John Adams's appeals to "Providence" are not "overtly Christian" (61). For similarly problematic assertions, usually involving qualifiers such as "uniquely," "overtly," "decidedly," and "distinctly," see pages 100, 131–33, 136, 179, and 245.

50. A great deal has been written about whether Washington believed in the divinity of Jesus Christ. But this controversy is unrelated to my point above, since the question is not what Washington believed, but how his readers would have interpreted his admonition to imitate the "characteristics of the Divine Author of our blessed religion."

51. To be clear, my argument is not that Washington's and Adams's references are, in fact, distinctly or uniquely Christian. One can imagine, for instance, a Muslim civic leader in an Islamic country making a statement that would be accurately translated as an appeal to "Providence." My contention is that their intended audiences would have understood Adams to be referring to the Christian God and Washington to be referring to His Son, Jesus Christ.

52. See Matthew Spalding and Patrick J. Garrity, *A Sacred Union of Citizens: George Washington's Farewell Address and the American Character* (Lanham: Rowman & Littlefield, 1998).

53. Dreisbach and Hall, *Sacred Rights of Conscience*, 468.

54. *The First Laws of the State of Connecticut*, ed. John D. Cushing (Wilmington: Michael Glazier, 1982), 184, see also 182–87.

55. Remarkably, despite all the evidence to the contrary, and without citing any evidence to support her claim, Brooke Allen simply asserts that the "framers, as a group, saw religion as a divisive rather than a cohesive force" (*Moral Minority*, 138). It is telling that, within a few pages of this statement, she

misidentifies Reverend James Willson as Bird Wilson (137); asserts that thirteen states sent representatives to the Constitutional Convention, when only twelve did (138); and states that Madison proposed two Religion Clauses in "the Constitutional Convention," when he proposed three concerning religion, all in the First Federal Congress (140). Like Matthew Stewart, Allen seems to be more interested in polemics than history.

56. See Plato, *The Republic*, trans. Desmond Lee, 2nd ed. (New York: Penguin, 1987).

57. Jean-Jacques Rousseau, *The Social Contract*, trans. Maurice Cranston (New York: Penguin, 1968).

58. Thomas Paine, *Common Sense and Other Political Writings*, ed. Nelson F. Adkins (New York: Macmillan, 1953), 31. For further discussion, see Cecelia M. Kenyon, "Where Paine Went Wrong," *American Political Science Review* 45 (December 1951): 1086–99, esp. 1094.

59. The Pennsylvania Constitution of 1776 is available at Yale Law School, Avalon Project, http://avalon.law.yale.edu/18th_century/pa08.asp; and that of 1790, https://www.duq.edu/academics/gumberg-library/pa-constitution/texts-of-the-constitution/1790 (both accessed July 30, 2018). Nebraska has a unicameral legislature, but its constitution contains a variety of checks on its power. Congress, under the Articles of Confederation, had so little power that there was little need for checks and balances.

60. "Lord Acton to Mandell Creighton, April 5, 1887," in *Historical Essays and Studies*, ed. J. N. Figgis and R. V. Laurence (London: Macmillan, 1907), 504.

61. Sydney E. Ahlstrom, *A Religious History of the American People* (Garden City: Doubleday, 1975), 1:426. See also Harry S. Stout, "Preaching the Insurrection," *Christian History* 15 (1996): 17; and Hall, *Roger Sherman*, 27–32.

62. *The New-England Primer*, ed. Paul Leicester Ford (1717; repr., New York: Dodd, Mead, and Co., 1897), 65.

63. Ralph Ketcham, *James Madison: A Biography* (Charlottesville: University Press of Virginia, 1971), 17–50.

64. Jeffry Morrison, *John Witherspoon and the Founding of the American Republic* (Notre Dame: University of Notre Dame Press, 2007), 4.

65. Marci A. Hamilton, "The Calvinist Paradox of Distrust and Hope at the Constitutional Convention," in *Christian Perspectives on Legal Thought*, ed. Michael W. McConnell, Robert F. Cochran Jr., and Angela C. Carmella (New Haven: Yale University Press, 2001), 293–306.

66. Farrand, *Records of the Federal Convention of 1787*, 1:20–23.
67. Farrand, *Records of the Federal Convention of 1787*, 1:133, 134.
68. Montesquieu, *The Spirit of the Laws*, ed. Anne Cohler, Basia Miller, and Harold Stone (Cambridge: Cambridge University Press, 1989).
69. Donald S. Lutz, "The Relative Influence of European Writers on Late Eighteenth-Century American Political Thought," *American Political Science Review* 78 (1984): 193. Locke is cited heavily in the 1760s and 1770s to justify resistance to Great Britain, and then he almost disappears from the literature. Montesquieu is most heavily cited during the 1780s, when many states and the new nation were drafting constitutions.
70. Madison might have concluded that men are self-interested for reasons that are not biblical or theological. He is a bit of an outlier in the founding generation for publicly, and accurately, acknowledging that religion can be a source of faction (see *Federalist* No. 10). But it seems likely to me that the Calvinists who educated him influenced his view of human nature.
71. Alexander Hamilton, James Madison, and John Jay, *The Federalist Papers*, ed. Clinton Rossiter (New York: New American Library, 1961), 315.
72. *Federalist Papers*, 322.
73. This is not to say that all students of the era recognize that the founders held this view. For instance, historian John Murrin wrote, "Quite possibly not a single delegate accepted Calvinist orthodoxy on original sin—that man is irretrievably corrupted and damned unless redeemed from outside." He goes on in the next sentence to observe that "Washington, Franklin, Madison, Hamilton, James Wilson, and Gouverneur Morris gave no sign of such a belief at this phase of their lives." It is telling that every founder he lists was either a lifelong Anglican or was worshipping in an Anglican church by the end of his life. If Murrin had looked at lifelong Calvinists in the era, he may have reached a different conclusion. Murrin, "Religion and Politics in America from the First Settlements to the Civil War," in Mark A. Noll, ed., *Religion and American Politics: From the Colonial Period to the 1980s* (New York: Oxford University Press, 1990), 31.
74. Barry Alan Shain, "Afterword: Revolutionary-Era Americans: Were They Enlightened or Protestant? Does It Matter?" in *The Founders on God and Government*, ed. Daniel L. Dreisbach, Mark D. Hall, and Jeffry H. Morrison (Lanham: Rowman & Littlefield, 2004), 275.
75. Shain, "Afterword: Revolutionary-Era Americans," 275.

76. Louis Hartz, "American Political Thought and the American Revolution," *American Political Science Review* 46 (June 1952): 324.

77. Brian Tierney, *The Idea of Natural Rights* (Grand Rapids: Eerdmans, 2001).

78. John Witte Jr., *The Reformation of Rights: Law, Religion, and Human Rights in Early Modern Calvinism* (Cambridge: Cambridge University Press, 2007).

79. *Collected Works of James Wilson*, ed. Kermit L. Hall and Mark David Hall (Indianapolis: Liberty Fund Press, 2007), 498.

80. On the willingness of Supreme Court justices to declare void laws that violate natural law, see Scott Douglas Gerber, ed., *Seriatim: The Early Supreme Court* (New York: NYU Press, 1998). I agree with Robert P. George, one of the finest natural law thinkers and students of jurisprudence in America today, that there are excellent reasons to deny jurists the ability to declare void a law that "is contrary to natural justice." George, "Natural Law, the Constitution, and the Theory and Practice of Judicial Review," in *Vital Remnants: America's Founding and the Western Tradition*, ed. Gary L. Gregg II (Wilmington: ISI, 1999), 168.

81. *Collected Works of James Wilson*, 498. For a detailed discussion of Wilson's view of natural law and natural rights, see Mark David Hall, *The Political and Legal Philosophy of James Wilson: 1742–1798* (Columbia: University of Missouri Press, 1997).

82. *Collected Works of James Wilson*, 1053–54.

83. See Sarah A. Morgan Smith and Mark David Hall, "Whose Rebellion? Reformed Resistance Theory in America, part 1," *Unio cum Christo* 3 (October 2017): 169–84, and "Whose Rebellion? Reformed Resistance Theory in America, part 2," *Unio cum Christo* 4 (April 2018): 171–88.

84. In a sequel to this book, I will argue that the American War of Independence was just and biblical.

85. Bruce Frohnen, *The American Republic* (Indianapolis: Liberty Fund Press, 2002), 15–22.

86. David D. Hall, *A Reforming People: Puritanism and the Transformation of Public Life in New England* (New York: Alfred A. Knopf, 2011), 148; and *The Book of the General Lawes and Libertyes Concerning the Inhabitants of Massachusetts* (1648; repr., San Marino: Huntington Library, 1998).

87. In Dreisbach and Hall, *Sacred Rights of Conscience*, 551–52. See also the anonymously published essay "Is Christianity a Part of the Common-Law of England?" in Dreisbach and Hall, *Sacred Rights of Conscience*, 552–59.

88. *Chisholm v. Georgia*, 2 U.S. 419 (1792), available in *Collected Works of James Wilson*, 353.

89. *Collected Works of James Wilson*, 590.

90. *Collected Works of James Wilson*, 1068.

91. *Collected Works of James Wilson*, 1067.

92. *Collected Works of James Wilson*, 1067.

93. *Collected Works of James Wilson*, 534.

94. *Collected Works of James Wilson*, 323.

95. William Blackstone, *Commentaries on the Laws of England: A Facsimile of the First Edition of 1765–1769* (Chicago: University of Chicago Press, 1979), http://press-pubs.uchicago.edu/founders/documents/amendIXs1.html. For a broader discussion of the founders and abortion, see Duane L. Ostler, "Abortion: What the Founding Fathers Thought About It," *Regent Journal of Law & Public Policy* 6 (Spring 2014): 181–218.

96. *Griswold v. Connecticut*, 381 U.S. 479 (1965). *Roe's* central holding was reaffirmed in *Planned Parenthood v. Casey*, 505 U.S. 833 (1992).

97. Wilson did write that unborn babies were protected by law once they are "first able to stir in the womb." But it seems likely that he would agree that they should be protected from the point of conception if he had had the scientific information we have now. For an excellent argument along these lines, see Hadley Arkes, *Natural Rights & the Right to Choose* (New York: Cambridge University Press, 2002).

98. Farrand, *Records of the Federal Convention of 1787*, 2:364.

99. See, for instance, Thomas G. West, *Vindicating the Founders: Race, Sex, and Justice in the Origins of America* (Lanham: Rowman & Littlefield, 1997), 1–36.

100. For many additional examples, see Dreisbach, *Reading the Bible*, 189–204. Ordered by the Pennsylvania Assembly in 1751, the Liberty Bell was known as the State House Bell until the nineteenth century. But it has come to be viewed as an important symbol of America's commitment to liberty.

101. See, for instance, Gregg L. Frazer, *The Religious Beliefs of America's Founders: Reason, Revelation, and Revolution* (Lawrence: University Press of Kansas, 2012), 7, 81; and Fea, *Was America Founded as a Christian Nation?*, 113.

102. *Pennsylvania Packet and Daily Advertiser*, December 25, 1790.

103. *Collected Works of James Wilson*, 435.

104. For an excellent discussion of the founders' views of liberty, see Barry Alan

Shain, *The Myth of American Individualism: The Protestant Origins of American Political Thought* (Princeton: Princeton University Press, 1994), 155–328; and Dreisbach, *Reading the Bible*, 200–204.

105. *Cohen v. California*, 403 U.S. 15 (1971).

106. *Texas v. Johnson*, 491 U.S. 397 (1989).

107. *Miller v. California*, 413 U.S. 15 (1973). Technically, this case involved defining obscenity, but the practical effect of the Court's decision in this case is to protect the publication of obscene and pornographic works.

108. Leonard W. Levy, *Emergence of a Free Press* (New York: Oxford University Press, 1985).

109. See, for instance, John Stuart Mill, *On Liberty* (1859), http://oll.libertyfund .org/titles/mill-the-collected-works-of-john-stuart-mill-volume-xviii-essays -on-politics-and-society-part-i (accessed September 18, 2018).

110. "Ake Green Cleared over Gay Sermon," *Local*, November 29, 2005, https:// www.thelocal.se/20120216/2590.

111. Davis, *Religion and the Continental Congress*, 34.

112. Dreisbach and Hall, *Sacred Rights of Conscience*, 242.

113. Dreisbach and Hall, *Sacred Rights of Conscience*, 373. It should be emphasized that Article VI did not affect religious tests for state and local offices. Daniel L. Dreisbach has argued that one purpose of the federal test ban may have been to protect these tests. Dreisbach, "The Constitution's Forgotten Religion Clause: Reflections on the Article VI Religious Test Ban," *Journal of Church and State* (Spring 1996): 261–95.

114. Dreisbach and Hall, *Sacred Rights of Conscience*, 388, 394.

115. Dreisbach and Hall, *Sacred Rights of Conscience*, 378. I suspect Ellsworth overstated his opposition to such tests because he wanted the Constitution to be ratified without delay. Williams responded that Ellsworth's logic would "apply with equal force against requiring an oath from any officer of the united or individual states" (380), a position Ellsworth never embraced. For more on Ellsworth, see my chapter, "Roger Sherman and Oliver Ellsworth," in *Great Christian Jurists in American History*, ed. Daniel L. Dreisbach and Mark David Hall (New York: Cambridge University Press, 2019).

116. Jonathan Elliott, ed., *The Debates in the Several State Conventions*, 2nd ed. (Washington, DC, 1836), 4:200.

117. Article XXXII of the North Carolina Constitution of 1776 is available at

Yale Law School, Avalon Project, http://avalon.law.yale.edu/18th_century
/nc07.asp (accessed February 26, 2018).

118. Henry's speech is reprinted in Jonathan D. Sarna and David G. Dalin,
Religion and State in the American Jewish Experience (Notre Dame: University
of Notre Dame Press, 1997), 83–85.

119. Article VI, Section 8, of the North Carolina Constitution of 1971 is
available at https://www.ncleg.net/Legislation/constitution/ncconstitution.
html (accessed August 25, 2018). The US Supreme Court declared all state
religious tests for civic office to be unconstitutional in *Torcaso v. Watkins*, 367
U.S. 488 (1961).

120. Dreisbach and Hall, *Sacred Rights of Conscience*, 390, 392, 397.

121. Justin McCarthy, "In U.S., Socialist Presidential Candidates Least Appealing,"
June 22, 2015, Gallup News, https://news.gallup.com/poll/183713/socialist
-presidential-candidates-least-appealing.aspx.

Chapter 3: Thomas Jefferson, James Madison, and the First Amendment

1. Forrest Church, ed., *The Separation of Church and State: Writings on a
Fundamental Freedom by America's Founders* (Boston: Beacon, 2004), xiii;
R. Freeman Butts, *The American Tradition in Religion and Education* (Boston:
Beacon, 1950), 3; Steven Waldman, *Founding Faith: Providence, Politics, and
the Birth of Religious Freedom in America* (New York: Random House, 2008),
xiii; Irving Brant, *James Madison: Father of the Constitution, 1787–1800*
(Indianapolis: Bobbs-Merrill, 1950), 272; and Leonard W. Levy, *Origins of the
Bill of Rights* (New Haven: Yale University Press, 1999), 86.

See also Mark Weldon Whitten, *The Myth of Christian America*
(Macon: Smyth & Helwys, 1999), 21 ("Madison was the driving force behind
the creation and adoption of the Bill of Rights . . . as President, [he] practiced
a strict separation of church and state"); Earl Warren, *Flast v. Cohen*, 392
U.S. 83 (1968), 103 ("James Madison, who is generally recognized as the
leading architect of the Religion Clauses of the First Amendment . . ."); Bill
Press, *How the Republicans Stole Christmas: The Republican Party's Declared
Monopoly on Religion and What Democrats Can Do to Take It Back* (New
York: Doubleday, 2005), 34 ("Inspired by Thomas Jefferson and written by
James Madison, [the Religion Clauses establish] the separation of church
and state"); Robert J. Morgan, *James Madison on the Constitution and the
Bill of Rights* (New York: Greenwood Press, 1988), 149 ("Madison called

for a strict separation of church and state for the additional reason that
he distrusted appeals to irrational sources of authority in the American
republic"); Frank Lambert, *Separation of Church and State: Founding Principle
of Religious Liberty* (Macon: Mercer University Press, 2014), 142 ("Inspired
by Enlightenment ideas of free enquiry, Jefferson used his reason to argue
that government ought to have nothing to do with religious matters other
than to guarantee religious liberty"); Richard Labunski, *James Madison and
the Struggle for the Bill of Rights* (New York: Oxford University Press, 2006),
256 ("Through the extraordinary efforts of a small man with a quiet voice,
the nation finally had the Bill of Rights"); and Geoffrey R. Stone, *Sex and the
Constitution: Sex, Religion, and Law from America's Origins to the Twenty-First
Century* (New York: W. W. Norton, 2017), 127 ("It was Thomas Jefferson,
however, who first crystallized the central meaning of the Establishment
Clause [as] . . . 'building a wall of separation between church and state'").

2. *Everson v. Board of Education*, 330 U.S. 1 (1947).
3. See, for instance, Justice John Paul Stevens's dissenting opinion in *Zelman v. Simmons-Harris*, 536 U.S. 639 (2002), 684–86.
4. Frederick Mark Gedicks and Rebecca G. Van Tassell, "RFRA Exceptions from the Contraception Mandate: An Unconstitutional Accommodation of Religion," *Harvard Civil Rights–Civil Liberties Law Review* 49 (Summer 2014), 343–84.
5. Activist Michael Newdow has made this argument numerous times, including in the litigation that resulted in the Supreme Court decision of *Elk Grove Unified School District v. Newdow*, 542 U.S. 1 (2004). More recently, Newdow has been involved in challenging the inclusion of the phrase "so help me God" in America's naturalization oath, even though no one is forced to say these words if they object to doing so. See Raelian Movement, "Raelian Seeking US Citizenship Sues to Remove 'So Help Me God' from Oath," PR Newswire, May 7, 2018, https://www.prnewswire.com/news-releases/raelian-seeking-us-citizenship-sues-to-remove-so-help-me-god-from-oath-300642809.html.
6. *Everson v. Board of Education*, 33.
7. *Everson v. Board of Education*, 39, 31–44.
8. *Everson v. Board of Education*, 13.
9. *Everson v. Board of Education*, 18.
10. Daniel L. Dreisbach and Mark David Hall, eds., *The Sacred Rights of*

Conscience: Selected Readings on Religious Liberty and Church-State Relations in the American Founding (Indianapolis: Liberty Fund Press, 2009), 528.

11. For a detailed account of Jefferson's and Madison's influence on the First Amendment, see my essay "Madison's Memorial and Remonstrance, Jefferson's Statute for Religious Liberty, and the Creation of the First Amendment," *American Political Thought* 3 (Spring 2014): 32–63. For an overview of how Supreme Court justices have used history in their Religion Clause opinions, see my article "Jeffersonian Walls and Madisonian Lines: The Supreme Court's Use of History in Religion Clause Cases," *High Court Quarterly Review* 5 (2009): 109–53.

12. Philip Hamburger, *Separation of Church and State* (Cambridge: Harvard University Press, 2002).

13. Hamburger, *Separation*, 422–34, 463.

14. Hamburger, *Separation*, 451.

15. Leo Pfeffer, *God, Caesar, and the Constitution* (Boston: Beacon, 1974), 159.

16. Martin Marty, "The Virginia Statute Two Hundred Years Later," in *The Virginia Statute for Religious Freedom: Its Evolution and Consequences,* ed. Merrill D. Peterson and Robert C. Vaughan (New York: Cambridge University Press, 1988), 3.

17. William Lee Miller, *The First Liberty: Religion and the American Republic* (New York: Knopf, 1986), 1–150, 357–66.

18. Paul Lucas, *American Odyssey, 1607–1789* (New York: Prentice-Hall, 1984), 229.

19. *Religious Freedom Day Guidebook*, https://static1.squarespace.com/static /5ac7adc7ec4eb79e30e02023/t/5c1440bdb8a0454b6ac35814 /1544831169413/RFD+2018+Guidebook.pdf (accessed February 11, 2019), 2.

20. Barack Obama, "Presidential Proclamation—National Religious Freedom Day," January 15, 2010, White House, Washington, DC, https:// obamawhitehouse.archives.gov/realitycheck/the-press-office/presidential -proclamation-religious-freedom-day; and "Presidential Proclamation —National Religious Freedom Day," January 13, 2012, White House, Washington, DC, http://www.whitehouse.gov/the-press-office/2012/01/13 /presidential-proclamation-religious-freedom-day-2012.

21. David Hackett Fischer, *Historians' Fallacies: Toward a Logic of Historical Thought* (New York: Harper & Row, 1970), 166, see also 103–30, 164–242.

22. Dumas Malone, *Jefferson and His Time: Jefferson the Virginian* (New York: Little, Brown, 1946), 279.

23. Hall, "Madison's Memorial and Remonstrance, Jefferson's Statute for Religious Liberty, and the Creation of the First Amendment," 25. This essay contains a far more extensive discussion of the availability and influence (or lack thereof) of both the Virginia Statute and the Memorial and Remonstrance.

24. *Pennsylvania Herald*, February 4, 1786, 1.

25. *Connecticut Gazette*, February 27, 1786, 3.

26. Dreisbach and Hall, *Sacred Rights of Conscience*, 231–35. The first Bible published in America was printed in the Algonquin language in 1663.

27. John Swanwick, "Considerations on an Act of the Legislature of Virginia" (Philadelphia, 1786), iii, 7.

28. Swanwick, "Considerations on an Act of the Legislature of Virginia," 9.

29. Swanwick, "Considerations on an Act of the Legislature of Virginia," 8–9.

30. For a detailed account of these debates, see my essay "Madison's Memorial and Remonstrance, Jefferson's Statute for Religious Liberty, and the Creation of the First Amendment."

31. Dreisbach and Hall, *Sacred Rights of Conscience*, 236–38.

32. In April 1785, Congress debated an early version of the ordinance that would have set aside federal land for "the support of religion." This provision was eventually removed, but there is no evidence to suggest that Jefferson's draft statute played any role in this outcome. (Madison's Memorial obviously did not, as it had not yet been written.) *Journals of the Continental Congress, 1774–1789*, ed. Worthington C. Ford et al. (Washington, DC: Government Printing Office, 1904–37), 28:291–96 (hereinafter cited as *JCC*).

33. Quoted in "Nathan Dane to Daniel Webster, March 26, 1830," in Robert A. Rutland, *The Birth of the Bill of Rights* (New York: Collier, 1962), 109.

34. Dreisbach and Hall, *Sacred Rights of Conscience*, 246.

35. See "State Constitution—Bill of Rights," New Hampshire at a Glance, https://www.nh.gov/glance/bill-of-rights.htm; "Constitution of Vermont—July 4, 1786," Yale Law School, Avalon Project, http://avalon.law.yale.edu/18th_century/vt02.asp (both accessed February 9, 2019); *The First Laws of the State of Connecticut*, ed. John D. Cushing (Wilmington: Michael Glazier, 1982), 21–22; and Dreisbach and Hall, *Sacred Rights of Conscience*, 246.

36. Neil H. Cogan, ed., *The Complete Bill of Rights: Drafts, Debates, Sources, and Origins* (New York: Oxford University Press, 1997), 11–13.

37. The town of Bellingham, Massachusetts, proposed that the Virginia Statute be adopted as an alternative to Article III of the Massachusetts Constitution of 1780, but this possibility was rejected in favor of the version of Article III quoted above. See William G. McLoughlin, *New England Dissent: The Baptists and Separation of Church and State* (Cambridge: Harvard University Press, 1971), 1:619.

38. Dreisbach and Hall, *Sacred Rights of Conscience*, 219.

39. Dreisbach and Hall, *Sacred Rights of Conscience*, 472. Derek Davis notes that in an 1822 letter to Edward Livingston, after his retirement from public life, Madison remarked that he disapproved of Congress's decision to appoint and pay chaplains, but there is no evidence that he objected publicly at the time. In his otherwise exhaustive treatment of the subject, Davis neglects to note that Madison voted to pay the Confederation Congress's chaplains in 1788. Davis, *Religion and the Continental Congress, 1774–1789* (New York: Oxford University Press, 2000), 77.

40. Dreisbach and Hall, *Sacred Rights of Conscience*, 453–57, 473–74.

41. Hall, "Madison's Memorial and Remonstrance, Jefferson's Statute for Religious Liberty, and the Creation of the First Amendment," 32–63.

42. See, for instance, Mark J. Chadsey, "Thomas Jefferson and the Establishment Clause," *Akron Law Review* 40 (2007): 623–46.

43. James Hitchcock, *The Supreme Court and Religion in American Life* (Princeton: Princeton University Press, 2004), 22; John Fea, *Was America Founded as a Christian Nation?* (Louisville: Westminster John Knox, 2011), 210; and Leonard W. Levy, *Original Intent and the Framers' Constitution* (New York: Macmillan, 1988), 144.

44. Thomas Buckley, email message to author, February 12, 2012. Similarly, H. J. Eckenrode concludes that the "repeal of the incorporation act definitely marks the separation of church and state in Virginia." Eckenrode, *Separation of Church and State in Virginia* (Richmond: Virginia State Library, 1910), 129.

45. Dreisbach and Hall, *Sacred Rights of Conscience*, 250–52; and Daniel L. Dreisbach, "A New Perspective on Jefferson's Views on Church-State Relations: The Virginia Statute for Establishing Religious Freedom in its Legislative Context," *American Journal of Legal History* 35 (April 1991): 172–204.

46. Andy Olree, "James Madison and Legislative Chaplains," *Northwestern University Law Review* 102 (2008): 171.

47. Thomas Buckley, *Church and State in Revolutionary Virginia* (Charlottesville: University of Virginia Press, 1977), 36.

48. Buckley, *Church and State in Revolutionary Virginia*, 33–37, 60–61. See also Daniel L. Dreisbach, "George Mason's Pursuit of Religious Liberty in Revolutionary Virginia," *The Virginia Magazine of History and Biography* 108 (2000): esp. 21–25.

49. Dreisbach and Hall, *Sacred Rights of Conscience*, 252–53.

50. Dreisbach and Hall, *Sacred Rights of Conscience*, 309.

51. Dreisbach and Hall, *Sacred Rights of Conscience*, 309.

52. Dreisbach and Hall, *Sacred Rights of Conscience*, 311–12. It is possible that Madison made these religious arguments simply because he thought they would be persuasive, not because he believed them. But even if this was the case, that he thought they would be effective tells us a great deal about Virginia's political culture in the era.

53. *The Papers of James Madison*, ed. Robert Rutland, William Rachal, Barbara Ripel, and Fredrika Teute (Chicago: University of Chicago Press, 1973), 8:297–98.

54. Dreisbach and Hall, *Sacred Rights of Conscience*, 307–8.

55. Steven K. Green, *The Second Disestablishment: Church and State in Nineteenth-Century America* (New York: Oxford University Press, 2010), 40.

56. Daniel M. Calhoon, *Political Moderation in America's First Two Centuries* (New York: Cambridge University Press, 2009), 211–12.

57. *Papers of James Madison*, 8:295.

58. Robert Semple, *History of the Rise and Progress of the Baptists in Virginia* (self-pub., 1810), 435–44.

59. The editors of *Papers of James Madison* incorrectly state that the 1786 pamphlet, published by Thomas, attributed the Memorial to Madison (8:305).

60. *The Papers of George Mason, 1725–1792*, ed. Robert A. Rutland (Chapel Hill: University of North Carolina Press, 1970), 2:830–32.

61. Buckley, *Church and State in Revolutionary Virginia*, 136.

62. Buckley, *Church and State in Revolutionary Virginia*, 117; and John A. Ragosta, *Wellspring of Liberty: How Virginia's Religious Dissenters Helped Win the American Revolution and Secured Religious Liberty* (New York: Oxford University Press, 2010), 120.

63. Hall, "Madison's Memorial and Remonstrance, Jefferson's Statute for Religious Liberty, and the Creation of the First Amendment," esp. 51–54.

64. Hall, "Madison's Memorial and Remonstrance, Jefferson's Statute for Religious Liberty, and the Creation of the First Amendment," esp. 51–54.

65. Dreisbach and Hall, *Sacred Rights of Conscience*, 312.

66. Dreisbach and Hall, *Sacred Rights of Conscience*, 311.

67. *Walz v. Tax Commissioner*, 397 U.S. 644 (1973), 705 (Douglas dissenting). Douglas attached to his opinion the full text of Madison's Memorial.

68. *Flast v. Cohen*, 392 U.S. 83 (1968) (Earl Warren, for the Court).

69. *Arizona Christian School Tuition Organization v. Winn*, 563 U.S. 125 (2011) (Kagan, joined by Ginsburg, Breyer, and Sotomayor, dissenting).

70. *Trinity Lutheran Church v. Comer*, 582 U.S. ___ (2017) (Sotomayor, joined by Ginsburg, dissenting).

71. *Documentary History of the First Federal Congress, 1789–1791*, ed. Linda Grant De Pauw et al. (Baltimore: Johns Hopkins University Press, 1972–?), 3:283 (hereinafter cited as DHFFC).

72. *DHFFC*, 11:1208, 1212, 1233, 4:27–31.

73. Dreisbach and Hall, *Sacred Rights of Conscience*, 420–21.

74. Dreisbach and Hall, *Sacred Rights of Conscience*, 430; and *DHFFC*, 11:1292, 4:39.

75. *DHFFC*, 4:7.

76. *DHFFC*, 4:6–9, 35–48, 3:216–18, 228–29, 11:1292, 19:1430, 1827; and Rutland, *Birth of the Bill of Rights*, 194–221. For a fine discussion of Ellsworth's role on the conference committee, see William R. Casto, "Oliver Ellsworth's Calvinist Vision of Church and State in the Early Republic," in Daniel L. Dreisbach, Mark David Hall, and Jeffry Morrison, eds., *The Forgotten Founders on Religion and Public Life* (Notre Dame: University of Notre Dame Press, 2009), 65–100.

77. Hall, "Jeffersonian Walls and Madisonian Lines," 568–69.

78. Dreisbach and Hall, *Sacred Rights of Conscience*, 528.

79. Dreisbach and Hall, *Sacred Rights of Conscience*, 533–34. The letter was first referenced in the Free Exercise Clause case of *Reynolds v. United States*, 98 U.S. 145 (1879).

80. Daniel L. Dreisbach, *Thomas Jefferson and the Wall of Separation Between Church and State* (New York: NYU Press, 2002).

81. James Hutson, "Thomas Jefferson's Letter to the Danbury Baptists: A

Controversy Rejoined," *The William and Mary Quarterly* 56 (October 1999): 786. Hutson also notes that when Jefferson "retired from the presidency, he resumed his earlier habit of worshiping in the Albemarle County Courthouse" (788).

82. Quoted in Dreisbach, *Thomas Jefferson and the Wall of Separation Between Church and State*, 138, 139.

83. Dreisbach and Hall, *Sacred Rights of Conscience*, 251–52.

84. Dreisbach and Hall, *Sacred Rights of Conscience*, 229.

85. Dreisbach and Hall, *Sacred Rights of Conscience*, 229. According to Derek Davis, Jefferson "later suggested it as an alternative motto for the Great Seal of Virginia, and he later added it to his personal seal." Davis, *Religion and the Continental Congress*, 138.

86. Thompson translated the Old Testament from the Septuagint version of the Bible, which was written in Greek.

87. See, for example, Jon Meacham, *American Gospel: God, the Founding Fathers, and the Making of a Nation* (New York: Random House, 2006), 81–82.

88. Dreisbach and Hall, *Sacred Rights of Conscience*, 229–31.

89. Dreisbach and Hall, *Sacred Rights of Conscience*, 531.

90. Dreisbach and Hall, *Sacred Rights of Conscience*, 530.

91. Dreisbach and Hall, *Sacred Rights of Conscience*, 476. Jefferson may have thought that the federal government was not restricted by the First Amendment in the context of a treaty with Native Americans. Edwin S. Gaustad suggests several other good reasons why Jefferson might have concluded that the treaty was permissible in *Sworn on the Altar of God: A Religious Biography of Thomas Jefferson* (Grand Rapids: William B. Eerdmans, 1996), 100–102. In any case, Jefferson's willingness to submit the treaty to the Senate indicates that he wasn't the sort of extreme separationist contemporary separationists would like him to have been.

92. Dreisbach and Hall, *Sacred Rights of Conscience*, 597–610.

93. Dreisbach and Hall, *Sacred Rights of Conscience*, 611.

94. Dreisbach and Hall, *Sacred Rights of Conscience*, 611.

95. Dreisbach and Hall, *Sacred Rights of Conscience*, 614.

96. Dreisbach and Hall, *Sacred Rights of Conscience*, 219.

97. Olree, "James Madison and Legislative Chaplains," 171–72.

98. Olree, "James Madison and Legislative Chaplains," 154, 173–76; and Dreisbach and Hall, *Sacred Rights of Conscience*, 472.

99. Dreisbach and Hall, *Sacred Rights of Conscience*, 453–57, 473–74.

100. Hutson, "Thomas Jefferson's Letter to the Danbury Baptists," 788. For additional information about church services in the US Capitol, see https://www.loc.gov/exhibits/religion/rel06–2.html (accessed November 28, 2018). Church services are discussed at the top and middle of the page.

101. Dreisbach and Hall, *Sacred Rights of Conscience*, 458–59.

102. *Journal of the House of Representatives of the United States* (Washington: Gales and Seaton, 1826), 7:567. Note that Madison misquotes the First Amendment, which begins: "Congress shall make no law respecting an establishment of religion . . ."

103. For additional presidential actions that both confirm and call into question Madison's commitment to the strict separation of church and state, see Olree "James Madison and Legislative Chaplains," 183–87.

104. Dreisbach and Hall, *Sacred Rights of Conscience*, 589–93.

105. Dreisbach and Hall, *Sacred Rights of Conscience*, 594–95; cf. 596–97.

106. Dreisbach and Hall, *Sacred Rights of Conscience*, 613. See Daniel L. Dreisbach, ed., *Religion and Politics in the Early Republic: Jasper Adams and the Church-State Debate* (Lexington: University Press of Kentucky, 1996).

Chapter 4: The Founders Believed Civic Authorities Should Protect, Promote, and Encourage Religion and Morality

1. Jonathan D. Sassi, "American Religious Eclectic and Secular," in *Christian America: Perspectives on Our Religious Heritage*, ed. Daryl C. Cornett (Nashville: B&H, 2011), 131; Jon Butler, "Why Revolutionary America Wasn't a 'Christian Nation,'" in *Religion and the New Republic*, ed. James H. Hutson (Lanham: Rowman & Littlefield, 2000), 196; James F. Harris, *The Serpentine Wall: The Winding Boundary between Church and State in the United States* (New Brunswick: Transaction, 2013), xi–xii; Susan Jacoby, *Freethinkers: A History of American Secularism* (New York: Metropolitan Books, 2004), 28; and Richard Dawkins, *The God Delusion* (Boston: Houghton Mifflin, 2006), 41–42.

   See also Noah Feldman, *Divided by God: America's Church-State Problem—And What We Should Do About It* (New York: Farrar, Straus and Giroux, 2005), 49 ("It is therefore historically inaccurate to claim that the Constitution, by banning an establishment of religion, allowed the government to support religion generally or nonpreferentially"); Derek

Davis, *Religion and the Continental Congress, 1774–1789* (New York: Oxford University Press, 2000), 227 ("All of the evidence, then, when examined in historical context, supports separationism as that paradigm of church-state thought that best captures the progressively evolving intentions of the founding fathers"); Richard T. Hughes, *Myths America Lives By* (Urbana: University of Illinois Press, 2003), 55 ("The First Amendment thereby provided the classic American doctrine of separation of church and state"); and Frank Lambert, *The Founding Fathers and the Place of Religion in America* (Princeton: Princeton University Press, 2003), 221 ("Many Americans, including the most influential Revolutionary leaders and members of the fastest-growing sects, called for the complete separation of church and state as the only sure safeguard of religious liberty").

2. The founders regularly used the word *religion* instead of *Christianity*, so I do as well throughout this chapter. On this point, see my essay "America's Founders, Religious Liberty, and the Common Good," *University of St. Thomas Law Journal* 15 (2019): 642–61.

3. There is no single, accepted definition of what it means to have an established church. Usually, establishments involve a state or nation favoring a particular denomination, often providing tax dollars to support it. A plural or multiple establishment generally requires individuals to support a church of their choosing. Michael McConnell, "Establishment and Disestablishment at the Founding, Part I: Establishment of Religion," *William and Mary Law Review* 44 (April 2003): 2131. For a discussion of different forms establishments may take, in both America and other countries, see J. Christopher Soper, Kevin R. den Dulk, and Stephen V. Monsma, *The Challenge of Pluralism: Church and State in Six Democracies*, 3rd ed. (Lanham: Rowman & Littlefield, 2017).

4. Daniel L. Dreisbach and Mark David Hall, eds., *The Sacred Rights of Conscience: Selected Readings on Religious Liberty and Church-State Relations in the American Founding* (Indianapolis: Liberty Fund Press, 2009), 242–64; John K. Wilson, "Religion Under the State Constitutions, 1776–1800," *The Journal of Church and State* 32 (Autumn 1990): 764; Derek Davis, *Religion and the Continental Congress, 1774–1789* (New York: Oxford University Press, 2000), 34; and Gerard V. Bradley, "The No Religious Test Clause and the Constitution of Religious Liberty: A Machine That Has Gone of Itself," *Case Western Law Review* 37 (1987): 681–87.

5. *Laws of the State of New York* (Albany, 1886), 2:637; and James S. Kabala,

Church-State Relations in the Early American Republic, 1787–1846 (London: Pickering & Chatto, 2013), 94–95.

6. Rhode Island never had an established church, but even this colony didn't completely separate church and state. For instance, in 1647, its General Court passed statutes punishing witchcraft and sodomy, citing Saint Paul in support of the latter. That Rhode Island was intended to be a place of liberty, not license, is evidenced by the last sentence of its criminal laws, which encourages all men to "walk as their consciences persuade them, every one in the name of his God; and let the saints of the Most High walk in this colony without molestation, in the name of Jehovah their God, for ever and ever." *The Earliest Acts and Laws of the Colony of Rhode Island and Providence Plantations, 1647–1719*, ed. John D. Cushing (Wilmington: Michael Glazier, 1977), 21, 25, 44. William G. McLoughlin reports that Seventh Day Baptists in the state "petitioned the legislature in 1784 for the repeal of a law requiring all persons to attend church on Sunday; the petition was granted, but the existence of the law in that state dominated by Baptists and Quakers indicated the pervasiveness of the belief that the Sabbath must be kept holy." McLoughlin, *New England Dissent: The Baptists and Separation of Church and State* (Cambridge: Harvard University Press, 1971), 2:758.

7. A good overview of church-state relations in America from the colonial era to the passage of the First Amendment may be found in Thomas J. Curry, *The First Freedoms: Church and State in America to the Passage of the First Amendment* (New York: Oxford University Press, 1986). See also the introductions to each chapter and the primary sources documents collected in Dreisbach and Hall, *Sacred Rights of Conscience*.

8. Of course, academic specialists are familiar with Sherman, and if you read books such as this one you probably know something about him. But by no stretch of the imagination is he as famous as Franklin, Washington, Adams, Jefferson, Madison, or Hamilton.

9. David Brian Robertson, "Madison's Opponents and Constitutional Design," *American Political Science Review* 99 (May 2005): 225–43, 242.

10. I provide an extensive account of these revisions in *Roger Sherman and the Creation of the American Republic* (New York: Oxford University Press, 2013), 77–91.

11. *The First Laws of the State of Connecticut*, ed. John D. Cushing (Wilmington: Michael Glazier, 1982), 233–35.

12. *First Laws of the State of Connecticut*, 21–22.

13. *First Laws of the State of Connecticut*, 8, 21–22, 41, 43, 67, 87, 89, 97, 101, 157–60, 182–87, 196–97, 213–14, 235–37, 258–59.

14. *First Laws of the State of Connecticut*, 21–22, 213–14.

15. Christopher Collier, "Common Law and Individual Rights in Connecticut Before the Federal Bill of Rights," *Connecticut Bar Journal* 76 (2002): 4.

16. *First Laws of the State of Connecticut*, 196–97. Connecticut did have a law that prohibited someone raised a Christian who later repudiated key tenets of his faith from holding civic office. Taken literally, this statute does not prevent a lifelong atheist or Jew from holding office, but the chances of this occurring in eighteenth-century Connecticut were virtually nonexistent (67).

17. *First Laws of the State of Connecticut*, 182–83.

18. On Ellsworth, see Mark David Hall, "Oliver Ellsworth: A Young Puritan in the New Republic," *Law and Liberty*, March 27, 2017, http://www.libertylawsite.org/2017/03/27/oliver-ellsworth-a-young-puritan-in-the-new-republic/.

19. Dreisbach and Hall, *Sacred Rights of Conscience*, 116–19.

20. Dreisbach and Hall, *Sacred Rights of Conscience*, 242. This is not to say that religious liberty was protected perfectly. See Jane E. Calvert, "Thomas Paine, Quakerism, and the Limits of Religious Liberty during the American Revolution," in *Selected Writings of Thomas Paine*, ed. Ian Shapiro and Jane E. Calvert (New Haven: Yale University Press, 2014), 602–29. Calvert also makes the point that Enlightenment radicals such as Paine were not always principled protectors of freedom of conscience.

21. Dreisbach and Hall, *Sacred Rights of Conscience*, 242.

22. Dreisbach and Hall, *Sacred Rights of Conscience*, 242.

23. Dreisbach and Hall, *Sacred Rights of Conscience*, 294–95.

24. Dreisbach and Hall, *Sacred Rights of Conscience*, 243.

25. R. Laurence Moore and Isaac Kramnick, *Godless Citizens in a Godly Republic: Atheists in American Public Life* (New York: W. W. Norton, 2018), 43.

26. *The First Laws of the Commonwealth of Pennsylvania*, ed. John D. Cushing (Wilmington: Michael Glazier, 1984), 181.

27. *First Laws of the Commonwealth of Pennsylvania*, 185.

28. *First Laws of the Commonwealth of Pennsylvania*, 282.

29. Lambert, *Founding Fathers and the Place of Religion*, 315.

30. Dreisbach and Hall, *Sacred Rights of Conscience*, 244.

31. See my essay "A Connecticut Yankee in Georgia: Abraham Baldwin and the Establishment Clause," *Law and Liberty*, October 18, 2018, https://www.lawliberty.org/2018/10/18/a-connecticut-yankee-in-georgia-abraham-baldwin-and-the-establishment-clause/.

32. Mark J. Chadsey, "Abraham Baldwin and the Establishment Clause," *Journal of Catholic Legal Studies* 51 (2012): 20–27.

33. Quoted in Chadsey, "Abraham Baldwin and the Establishment Clause," 31.

34. *The First Laws of the State of Georgia*, ed. John D. Cushing (Wilmington: Michael Glazier, 1981), 1:299.

35. *First Laws of the State of Georgia*, 301.

36. *First Laws of the State of Georgia*, 301.

37. *The Colonial Records of the State of Georgia*, ed. Lucian Lamar Knight, Kenneth Coleman, and Milton Ready (Atlanta: Charles P. Byrd, 1911), 91; part 2, 395.

38. *Colonial Records of the State of Georgia*, 397.

39. *Colonial Records of the State of Georgia*, 395–96.

40. Chadsey, "Abraham Baldwin and the Establishment Clause," 34.

41. *Colonial Records of the State of Georgia*, 489.

42. Some proponents of church-state separation believe that this trend continued unabated until Massachusetts disestablished its church in 1833, but careful students of the subject recognize that the proper relationship between church and state has been hotly contested throughout American history. See, for instance, Steven K. Green, *The Second Disestablishment: Church and State in Nineteenth-Century America* (New York: Oxford University Press, 2010), and Kabala, *Church-State Relations in the Early American Republic*. For a discussion of the debates over disestablishment in every state, see Jonathan Den Hartog and Carl Esbeck, eds., *Religious Dissent and Disestablishment: Church-State Relations in the New American States, 1776–1833* (Columbia: University of Missouri Press, 2019).

43. Davis, *Religion and the Continental Congress*, 35. Most states eventually and voluntarily removed their religious tests for office, and the few remaining tests were declared unconstitutional in *Torcaso v. Watkins*, 367 U.S. 488 (1961).

44. Dreisbach and Hall, *Sacred Rights of Conscience*, 216.

45. Dreisbach and Hall, *Sacred Rights of Conscience*, 216.

46. Dreisbach and Hall, *Sacred Rights of Conscience*, 216.

47. Davis, *Religion and the Continental Congress*, 75–77; *Journals of the*

Continental Congress, 1774–1789, ed. Worthington C. Ford et al. (Washington, DC: Government Printing Office, 1904–37), 5:530, 887 (hereinafter cited as *JCC*); and Ida A. Brudnick, "House and Senate Chaplains: An Overview," *Congressional Research Service Report*, May 26, 2011.

48. Davis, *Religion and the Continental Congress*, 80–81.

49. Quoted in Davis, *Religion and the Continental Congress*, 81.

50. *The Public Records of Connecticut* (Hartford: Case, Lockwood and Brainard, 1894), 15:22. Connecticut's law was patterned after a similar one passed by Massachusetts. *Journal of the Provincial Congress of Massachusetts* (April 5, 1775): 12.

51. *JCC*, 2:112.

52. Dreisbach and Hall, *Sacred Rights of Conscience*, 217.

53. Davis, *Religion and the Continental Congress*, 86. See also Ann Fairfax Withington, *Toward a More Perfect Union: Virtue and the Formation of America Republics* (New York: Oxford University Press, 1991).

54. Dreisbach and Hall, *Sacred Rights of Conscience*, 224.

55. *JCC*, 11:481.

56. *JCC*, 11:481.

57. On Witherspoon, see Jeffry Morrison, *John Witherspoon and the Founding of the American Republic* (Notre Dame: University of Notre Dame Press, 2007).

58. *JCC*, 21:1076.

59. Dreisbach and Hall, *Sacred Rights of Conscience*, 235–36.

60. *JCC*, 1:78.

61. Dreisbach and Hall, *Sacred Rights of Conscience*, 225–26.

62. See, for example, *JCC*, 12:1001–3.

63. Dreisbach and Hall, *Sacred Rights of Conscience*, 234–35.

64. Dreisbach and Hall, *Sacred Rights of Conscience*, 231.

65. "John Sullivan to George Washington, July 2, 1781," in *Letters of the Members of the Continental Congress*, ed. Edmund C. Burnett (Washington, DC: Carnegie Institution, 1933), 6:133.

66. Dreisbach and Hall, *Sacred Rights of Conscience*, 472–73.

67. Dreisbach and Hall, *Sacred Rights of Conscience*, 236–38, 473. In April 1785, Congress debated an early version of the ordinance that would have set aside federal land for "the support of religion." This provision was eventually removed, and the language quoted was adopted in its place. The ordinance does not clearly require government support for religion and/or

religious education, but it leaves the door open for this possibility. *JCC*, 28:293–96.

68. Dreisbach and Hall, *Sacred Rights of Conscience*, 472.

69. *Documentary History of the First Federal Congress, 1789–1791*, ed. Linda Grant De Pauw et al. (Baltimore: Johns Hopkins University Press, 1972–?), 11:1500–1501 (hereinafter cited as *DHFFC*). Additional actions taken by early Congresses that supported or encouraged faith are discussed in chapter 3 of this book, and in Dreisbach and Hall, *Sacred Rights of Conscience*, 473–76.

70. Dreisbach and Hall, *Sacred Rights of Conscience*, 453–54.

71. See, for instance, Michael I. Meyerson, *Endowed by Our Creator: The Birth of Religious Liberty in America* (New Haven: Yale University Press, 2012), 181–82. Ed Asner is an interesting exception to this rule. He concedes, without offering any evidence, that Washington said "so help me God" when he took the oath, but then explains that he did so because he was a Mason and "that's how *every* Mason ends his oath." He concludes that the phrase is "Masonic and not God-inspired." Ed Asner and Ed. Weinberger, *Grouchy Historian: An Old-Time Lefty Defends Our Constitution Against Right-Wing Hypocrites and Nutjobs* (New York: Simon & Schuster, 2017), 33. Asner is correct that Masons routinely ended oaths by saying "so help me God" (and kissing the Bible), but these were deeply ingrained Christian practices. Asner's treatment of this and related issues suggests that being a television star (he is best known for playing Lou Grant on *The Mary Tyler Moore Show*) may not prepare one well for writing about American history. For a good discussion of these matters by someone who is not a professional actor, see Frederick B. Jonassen, "Kiss the Book . . . You're President. . . . : 'So Help Me God' and Kissing the Book in the Presidential Oath of Office," *William and Mary Bill of Rights Journal* 20 (2012): 853–953.

72. Dreisbach and Hall, *Sacred Rights of Conscience*, 444.

73. For detailed documentation of this point, see my essay "Madison's Memorial and Remonstrance, Jefferson's Statute for Religious Liberty, and the Creation of the First Amendment," *American Political Thought* 3 (Spring 2014): 55.

74. Forrest Church reached a similar conclusion for slightly different reasons in *So Help Me God: The Founding Fathers and the First Great Battle Over Church and State* (New York: Harcourt, 2007), 445–49. See also Daniel L. Dreisbach, *Reading the Bible with the Founding Fathers* (New York: Oxford University Press, 2017), 205–10.

75. Dreisbach and Hall, *Sacred Rights of Conscience*, 456.

76. Dreisbach and Hall, *Sacred Rights of Conscience*, 457.

77. Dreisbach, *Reading the Bible*, 145–58.

78. See, for example, Michael I. Meyerson, "The Original Meaning of 'God': Using the Language of the Framing Generation to Create a Coherent Establishment Clause Jurisprudence," *Marquette Law Review* 98 (2015): 1092–94.

79. As discussed in the previous chapter, President Jefferson refused to issue formal calls for prayer, but he urged citizens to pray in his other addresses. Madison almost certainly did not want to issue formal calls for prayer, but he did so anyway. Every other president, with the exception of Andrew Jackson, has issued calls for prayer. Davis, *Religion and the Continental Congress*, 90.

80. *Engel v. Vitale*, 370 U.S. 421 (1962). The Court's conclusion is not required as a matter of original understanding, but there are good prudential reasons for not having teacher-led prayer in public schools today. Fortunately, the Supreme Court recognizes that public school students have every right to gather voluntarily for prayer, Bible study, and other religious activities. An excellent collection of resources on these issues is available at "Resources for Teachers," Christian Legal Society Center for Law and Religious Freedom, https://www.clsreligiousfreedom.org/teacherresources (accessed February 21, 2019).

81. "United States Oracle, May 24, 1800," in *The Documentary History of the Supreme Court of the United States, 1789–1800*, ed. Maeva Marcus (New York: Columbia University Press, 1990), 3:436.

82. Dreisbach and Hall, *Sacred Rights of Conscience*, 473.

83. Harris, *The Serpentine Wall*, 78–79; Anson Phelps Stokes made a similar claim in his *Church and State in the United States* (New York: Harper & Brothers, 1950), 1:492.

84. Dreisbach and Hall, *Sacred Rights of Conscience*, 476.

85. Brooke Allen, *Moral Minority: Our Skeptical Founding Fathers* (Chicago: Ivan R. Dee, 2006), 142.

86. Harris, *The Serpentine Wall*, 78–81; Lambert, *Founding Fathers and the Place of Religion*, 238–41; Hughes, *Myths America Lives By*, 66; Martha C. Nussbaum, *Liberty of Conscience: In Defense of America's Tradition of Religious Equality* (New York: Basic Books, 2008), 113; Gregg L. Frazer, *The*

Religious Beliefs of America's Founders: Reason, Revelation, and Revolution
(Lawrence: University Press of Kansas, 2012), 234. See also Mark A. Noll,
Nathan O. Hatch, and George M. Marsden, *The Search for Christian America*
(Westchester: Crossway, 1983), 131; Robert Boston, *Why the Religious
Right Is Wrong About Separation of Church and State*, 2nd ed. (Amherst:
Prometheus Books, 2003), 253; Bill Press, *How the Republicans Stole
Christmas: The Republican Party's Declared Monopoly on Religion and What
Democrats Can Do to Take It Back* (New York: Doubleday, 2005), 52; Stokes,
Church and State in the United States, 1:497–98; and Dawkins, *The God
Delusion*, 40.

87. "American Commissioners to John Jay, March 28, 1786," The US National
Archives and Records Administration, https://founders.archives
.gov/?q=laws%20of%20their%20Prophet%2C%20that%20it%20was%20
written%20in%20their%20Koran&s=1111311111&r=1 (accessed February
21, 2019).

88. Four years after the treaty was ratified, Secretary of War James McHenry
wrote to the secretary of the treasury that he was outraged by Article 11.
Perhaps this is one reason it was excised from future versions of the treaty. See
Meyerson, *Endowed by Our Creator*, 201.

89. Frank Lambert, *The Barbary Wars: American Independence in the Atlantic
World* (New York: Hill and Wang, 2007). John Fea, who often highlights
evidence that suggests America was not founded as a Christian nation,
recognizes that it is a mistake to take the Treaty of Tripoli as a principled
statement of church-state relations. Fea, *Was America Founded as a Christian
Nation?* (Louisville: Westminster John Knox, 2011), 3–4.

90. Dreisbach and Hall, *Sacred Rights of Conscience*, 253–54.

91. Dreisbach and Hall, *Sacred Rights of Conscience*, 252.

92. Quoted in Philip Hamburger, *Separation of Church and State* (Cambridge:
Harvard University Press, 2002), 69.

93. Dreisbach and Hall, *Sacred Rights of Conscience*, 307.

94. Dreisbach and Hall, *Sacred Rights of Conscience*, 307–8.

95. Dreisbach and Hall, *Sacred Rights of Conscience*, 308.

96. Dreisbach and Hall, *Sacred Rights of Conscience*, 311–12.

97. Dreisbach and Hall, *Sacred Rights of Conscience*, 313.

98. Dreisbach and Hall, *Sacred Rights of Conscience*, 250.

99. Dreisbach and Hall, *Sacred Rights of Conscience*, 468.

Chapter 5: Christianity, Religious Liberty, and Religious Exemptions

1. Frank Lambert, *Separation of Church and State: Founding Principle of Religious Liberty* (Macon: Mercer University Press, 2014), 142; David L. Holmes, *The Faiths of the Founding Fathers* (New York: Oxford University Press, 2006), 22; Gregg L. Frazer, *The Religious Beliefs of America's Founders: Reason, Revelation, and Revolution* (Lawrence: University Press of Kansas, 2012), 220; and Jon Butler, "Coercion, Miracle, Reason: Rethinking the American Religious Experience in the Revolutionary Age," in *Religion in a Revolutionary Age*, ed. Ronald Hoffman and Peter J. Albert (Charlottesville: University Press of Virginia, 1994), 29.

   See also Forrest Church, ed., *The Separation of Church and State: Writings on a Fundamental Freedom by America's Founders* (Boston: Beacon Press, 2004), xiii ("[Madison] became a dogged secular advocate of church-state separation"); Kenneth R. Craycraft Jr., *The American Myth of Religious Freedom* (Dallas: Spence Publishing, 1999), 69 ("If Locke was the great theorist of freedom of conscience and religion, Thomas Jefferson and James Madison were its great practitioners"); and Jack N. Rakove, *Original Meanings: Politics and Ideas in the Making of the Constitution* (New York: Vintage, 1997), 311 (". . . religious liberty that was so much the project of the Enlightenment").

2. Marci A. Hamilton, *God vs. the Gavel: Religion and the Rule of Law*, 2nd rev. ed. (New York: Cambridge University Press, 2015), 310; and Brian Leiter, *Why Tolerate Religion?* (Princeton: Princeton University Press, 2013), 4. At one level, Hamilton and Leiter are obviously correct. No founder thought that religious liberty permits believers to kill, rob, or rape in God's name, and appropriately so. But they oppose many existing accommodations that protect religious minorities.

3. Good secondary works that support this point include Thomas J. Curry, *The First Freedoms: Church and State in America to the Passage of the First Amendment* (New York: Oxford University Press, 1986); Andrew R. Murphy, *Conscience and Community: Revisiting Toleration and Religious Dissent in Early Modern England and America* (University Park: Penn State University Press, 2001); Anthony Gill, *The Political Origins of Religious Liberty* (New York: Cambridge University Press, 2008); and Nicholas Miller, *The Religious Roots of the First Amendment: Dissenting Protestants and the Separation of Church and State* (New York: Oxford University Press, 2012).

4. "England's Present Interest Considered" (1675), in Andrew R. Murphy, ed., *The Political Writings of William Penn* (Indianapolis: Liberty Fund Press, 2002), 57.

5. Murphy, *Political Writings of William Penn*, 340.

6. Daniel L. Dreisbach and Mark David Hall, eds., *The Sacred Rights of Conscience: Selected Readings on Religious Liberty and Church-State Relations in the American Founding* (Indianapolis: Liberty Fund Press, 2009), 115, 118. See also Roger Williams, "Charter of Rhode Island and Providence Plantation," (1663), http://avalon.law.yale.edu/17th_century/ri04.asp.

7. Richard Bauman, *For the Reputation of Truth: Politics, Religion, and Conflict Among the Pennsylvania Quakers: 1750–1800* (Baltimore: Johns Hopkins University Press, 1971), 1–15.

8. See, for instance, Murphy, *Political Writings of William Penn*, 62–74, 99–101, 126.

9. Isaac Backus, *An Appeal to the Public for Religious Liberty* (1773), in Ellis Sandoz, ed., *Political Sermons of the American Founding Era, 1735–1805*, 2nd ed. (Indianapolis: Liberty Fund Press, 1998), 359.

10. Dreisbach and Hall, *Sacred Rights of Conscience*, 274.

11. Dreisbach and Hall, *Sacred Rights of Conscience*, 275, 273–76.

12. Dreisbach and Hall, *Sacred Rights of Conscience*, 270.

13. Dreisbach and Hall, *Sacred Rights of Conscience*, 395.

14. Dreisbach and Hall, *Sacred Rights of Conscience*, 175.

15. Williams's references to Locke are used by scholars who claim that ministers in the founding era abandoned their commitment to Christian political ideas and substituted in their place largely secular political ones. See, for instance, Michael R. Zuckert, *The Natural Rights Republic* (Notre Dame: University of Notre Dame Press, 1996), 172, 183–93. I respond to this claim in *Roger Sherman and the Creation of the American Republic* (New York: Oxford University Press, 2013), esp. 1–40.

16. Dreisbach and Hall, *Sacred Rights of Conscience*, 178.

17. Dreisbach and Hall, *Sacred Rights of Conscience*, vii, 459. To be sure, there was the obvious political motive of attempting to convince Catholic Quebec to enter the War of Independence on the patriot side. Many states retained anti-Catholic laws (or added them) well into the early twentieth century. Derek Davis, *Religion and the Continental Congress, 1774–1789* (New York: Oxford University Press, 2000), 153.

18. Dreisbach and Hall, *Sacred Rights of Conscience*, 459, vii–viii.
19. Dreisbach and Hall, *Sacred Rights of Conscience*, 241.
20. Dreisbach and Hall, *Sacred Rights of Conscience*, 241. See Daniel L. Dreisbach, "George Mason's Pursuit of Religious Liberty in Revolutionary Virginia," *The Virginia Magazine of History and Biography* 108 (2000): 5–44.
21. Backus, *Appeal to the Public for Religious Liberty*, 339.
22. Backus, *Appeal to the Public for Religious Liberty*, 339, and generally, 331–68.
23. Dreisbach and Hall, *Sacred Rights of Conscience*, 276.
24. Dreisbach and Hall, *Sacred Rights of Conscience*, 337.
25. Dreisbach and Hall, *Sacred Rights of Conscience*, 246.
26. This is not to say America's founders *only* made Christian arguments, but, as I have argued elsewhere in this book, when they appealed to other authorities, they almost always understood them to be compatible with orthodox Christianity. For a twenty-first-century evaluation of these arguments by a philosopher who reaches a conclusion similar to mine, see Nicholas Wolterstorff, "A Religious Argument for the Civil Right to Freedom of Religious Exercise, Drawn from American History," *Wake Forest Law Review* (Summer 2001): 535–56.
27. For a good overview, see Vincent Phillip Muñoz, "If Religious Liberty Does Not Mean Exemptions, What Might It Mean? The Founders' Constitutionalism of the Inalienable Rights of Religious Liberty," *Notre Dame Law Review* 91 (2016): 1387–418. Various religious liberty provisions are conveniently collected in Neil H. Cogan, ed., *The Complete Bill of Rights: Drafts, Debates, Sources, and Origins* (New York: Oxford University Press, 1997), 1–52. Of course, religious liberty was not protected perfectly. As discussed in chapter 4, many states continued to have religious tests for officeholders, and in an ill-conceived attempt to protect religion, seven states prohibited clergy from holding civic offices. Many Christians believe that ministers should not enter electoral politics, but it violates the rights of clergy to prohibit them from doing so as a matter of law. Most states voluntarily removed these restrictions, and the US Supreme Court declared the few remaining ones to be unconstitutional in *McDaniel v. Paty*, 435 U.S. 618 (1978).
28. Technically, Congress had the power to pass such laws for the federal territories, but instead of doing so, it guaranteed in the Northwest Ordinance (1789) that "No person demeaning himself in a peaceable and orderly

manner, shall ever be molested on account of his mode of worship or religious sentiments." Dreisbach and Hall, *Sacred Rights of Conscience*, 236, 473.

29. Dreisbach and Hall, *Sacred Rights of Conscience*, 433.

30. Only about half the states currently have statewide laws prohibiting discrimination on the basis of sexual orientation in public accommodations, and good arguments can be made that wedding service providers like Barronelle Stutzman were not discriminating on the basis of sexual orientation per se. For the purposes of this chapter, I assume for the sake of argument that these laws promote the common good. Examples of such cases include *Elane Photography, L.L.C v. Willock*, 2013-NMSC-040, 309 P.3d 53; *State of Washington v. Arlene's Flowers*, No. 13–2–008715, February 18, 2015; and *In the Matter of Melissa Elaine Klein, Interim Order, Commissioner of the Bureau of Labor and Industries*, Case nos. 44–14 and 45–14, January 29, 2015.

31. Part of this chapter was published as Mark David Hall, "Religious Accommodations and the Common Good," *The Heritage Foundation Backgrounder*, October 26, 2015, http://www.heritage.org/research/reports /2015/10/religious-accommodations-and-the-common-good.

32. Kelsey Harkness, "Q&A with Washington Florist," *Daily Signal*, April 10, 2015, https://www.dailysignal.com/2015/04/10/qa-with-washington-florist -on-religious-freedom-who-are-the-real-bigots-here/.

33. *State of Washington v. Arlene's Flowers*, No. 13–2–008715, February 18, 2015. Stutzman was defended by Austin R. Nimocks and other attorneys from the Alliance Defending Freedom. They asked me to be an expert witness in this case, a challenge I gladly accepted. But I never had the opportunity to testify because the trial judge issued a summary judgment against Stutzman. The expert report I wrote became the basis for my essay "Religious Accommodations and the Common Good."

34. Dreisbach and Hall, *Sacred Rights of Conscience*, 468.

35. James Endell Tyler, *Oaths; Their Origin, Nature, and History* (London: John W. Parker, 1834), 9–15.

36. "Reconsideration of the Sworn Testimony Requirement: Securing Truth in the Twentieth Century," *Michigan Law Review* 75 (1977): 1692.

37. *Records of the Colony of Rhode Island and Providence Plantations*, ed. John Russell Bartlett (Providence: Greene & Brother, 1856), 1:181–82.

38. See, for instance, Roger Williams, *George Fox Digged Out of His Burrowes* (1672).

39. Peter A. Waller, author of a two-volume biography on Pierce, passes over the oath ceremony without comment in his *Franklin Pierce: New Hampshire's Favorite Son* (Concord: Plaidswede Publishing, 2004), 1:252. In a radio interview, he responded to a question about the ceremony by saying that he did not know why Pierce decided to affirm rather than swear. Brady Carlson, "Franklin Pierce's Inaugural Day: Unique Touches and Great Challenges," New Hampshire Public Radio, January 21, 2013, http://nhpr.org/post /franklin-pierces-inaugural-day-unique-touches-and-great-challenges #stream/0.

40. Dreisbach and Hall, *Sacred Rights of Conscience*, 442. For specific biblical passages, see Mahita Gajanan, "These Are the Bible Verses Past Presidents Have Turned to on Inauguration Day," *Time*, January 9, 2017, http://time .com/4639596/inauguration-day-presidents-bible-passages/.

41. *The Documentary History of the Supreme Court of the United States, 1789–1800*, ed. Maeva Marcus (New York: Columbia University Press, 1990), 4:52–53, 421.

42. *Journals of the Continental Congress, 1774–1789*, ed. Worthington C. Ford et al. (Washington, DC: Government Printing Office, 1904–37), 2:189 (hereinafter cited as *JCC*).

43. Quoted in Hall, *Roger Sherman*, 139.

44. Hall, *Roger Sherman*, 139.

45. Hall, *Roger Sherman*, 144.

46. Hall, *Roger Sherman*, 145.

47. See my essay "Religious Accommodations and the Common Good," for more details on the development of how conscientious objectors have been treated by the federal government.

48. For example, see Frederick Mark Gedicks and Rebecca G. Van Tassell, "RFRA Exceptions from the Contraception Mandate: An Unconstitutional Accommodation of Religion," *Harvard Civil Rights–Civil Liberties Law Review* 49 (Summer 2014), 343–84. With one exception, the US Supreme Court has rejected the contention that accommodations violate the Establishment Clause. On this point, see Carl H. Esbeck, "Third-Party Burdens, Congressional Accommodations for Religion, and the Establishment Clause," a testimony given before the Judiciary Committee's subcommittee on the Constitution and Civil Justice, February 13, 2015.

49. There is an extensive scholarly debate over whether America's founders

intended for the Free Exercise Clause to require accommodations. See, for instance, Michael W. McConnell, "The Origins and Historical Understanding of Free Exercise of Religion," *Harvard Law Review* 103 (May 1990): 1409–517; Philip A. Hamburger, "A Constitutional Right of Religious Exemption: An Historical Perspective," *George Washington Law Review* 60 (April 1992): 915–48; Ellis M. West, "The Right to Religion-Based Exemptions in Early America: The Case of Conscientious Objectors to Conscription," *Journal of Law and Religion* 10 (1993–1994): 367–401; and Douglas Laycock, "The Religious Exemption Debate," *Rutgers Journal of Law & Religion* 11 (Fall 2009): 152–54.

50. *Sherbert v. Verner*, 374 U.S. 398 (1963).

51. Hall, "Religious Accommodations and the Common Good," 11–12.

52. Public Law 66–66, National Prohibition Act (Volstead Act), 66th Cong., 1st Sess., October 28, 1919, http://www.legisworks.org/congress/66/publaw-66.pdf (accessed September 3, 2015). See also *Gonzales v. O Centro Espirita Beneficente Uniao do Vegetal*, 546 U.S. 418 (2006), which held that RFRA protected the ability of members of a small Brazilian church to use hallucinogenic tea in religious ceremonies.

53. RFRA of 1993, Public Law 103–141, November 16, 1993, http://www.justice.gov/sites/default/files/jmd/legacy/2014/07/24/act-pl103-141.pdf.

54. *City of Boerne v. Flores*, 521 U.S. 507 (1997). Other states have not enacted such laws, in some cases because courts continue to interpret their state constitutions to require strict scrutiny of laws restricting religious activities. For a helpful compilation of state RFRAs, see "State Religious Freedom Restoration Acts," National Conference of State Legislatures, June 5, 2015, http://www.ncsl.org/research/civil-and-criminal-justice/state-rfra-statutes.aspx. Professor Robin Fretwell Wilson and her colleagues maintain a helpful website tracking legislation of this nature at the state level, https://robin-fretwellwilson.squarespace.com/maps-of-laws (accessed June 14, 2019).

55. In addition to the acts mentioned above, Congress also passed the Religious Liberty and Charitable Donation Protection Act (1998) and the Religious Land Use and Institutionalized Persons Act (2000).

56. Hamilton, *God vs. the Gavel*; Brian Leiter, *Why Tolerate Religion?*; John Corvino, Ryan T. Anderson, and Sherif Girgis, *Debating Religious Liberty and Discrimination* (New York: Oxford University Press, 2017), Corvino's

chapters; and Richard Schragger and Micah Schwartzman, "Against Religious Institutionalism," *Virginia Law Review* 99 (2013): 917–85.

57. Micah Schwartzman, "What If Religion Is Not Special?," *University of Chicago Law Review* 79 (2012): 1350–427. For an excellent response, see Christopher C. Lund, "Religion Is Special Enough," *Virginia Law Review* 103 (2017): 481–524.

58. *Burwell v. Hobby Lobby Stores*, 573 U.S. ___ (2014).

59. US Commission on Civil Rights, "Peaceful Coexistence: Reconciling Nondiscrimination Principles with Civil Liberties" (September 2016): 29, https://www.usccr.gov/pubs/docs/Peaceful-Coexistence-09–07–16.pdf.

60. For a discussion of this case and its impact, see my essay "A Missed Opportunity: *Masterpiece Cakeshop v. Colorado Civil Rights Commission*," *Law and Liberty*, June 6, 2018, http://www.libertylawsite.org/2018/06/06 /masterpiece-cakeshop-v-colorado-civil-rights-commission/.

61. American Civil Liberties Union, "ACLU Statement on the So-Called 'Religious Freedom' Executive Order," May 4, 2017, https://www.aclu.org /news/aclu-statement-so-called-religious-freedom-executive-order.

62. See "President Trump Has Been a Champion for Religious Freedom," February 8, 2018, https://www.whitehouse.gov/briefings-statements /president-trump-champion-religious-freedom/. Although this is hardly an unbiased list, it references easily verifiable executive orders and actions.

63. As of November 2018, President Trump has appointed two excellent US Supreme Court justices, and a host of lower federal court judges, who should be far more protective of religious freedom than jurists appointed by President Obama.

64. I am inclined to think these laws do more harm than good, but that is an argument for another day.

65. This sort of compromise is hardly original with me. See, for instance, Douglas Laycock and Thomas C. Berg, "Protecting Same-Sex Marriage and Religious Liberty," *Virginia Law Review* 99 (2013): 1–10, https://papers.ssrn.com/sol3 /papers.cfm?abstract_id=2254131##.

66. For an excellent collection of essays on this subject, see William N. Eskridge Jr. and Robin Fretwell Wilson, eds., *Religious Freedom, LGBT Rights, and the Prospects for the Common Good* (New York: Cambridge University Press, 2019).

67. *West Virginia v. Barnette*, 319 U.S. 624 (1943).

68. *Holt v. Hobbes*, 574 U.S. ___ (2015).
69. *Gonzales v. O Centro Espirita Beneficente Uniao do Vegetal*, 546 U.S. 418 (2006).
70. *Wisconsin v. Yoder*, 406 U.S. 205 (1972).
71. See, for instance, the 2017 survey by CATO Institute, https://www.cato.org /survey-reports/state-free-speech-tolerance-america#77 (accessed August 25, 2018); and Bryan Fischer, "Islam and the First Amendment: Privileges but Not Rights," RenewAmerica, March 24, 2011, http://www.renewamerica .com/columns/fischer/110324. Daniel Bennett, in *Defending Faith: The Politics of the Christian Conservative Legal Movement* (Lawrence: University Press of Kansas, 2017), shows that most conservative Christian legal advocacy groups understand the importance of protecting the religious liberty of all Americans. But, of course, not *all* convictions should be protected. For instance, I have argued (with coauthor Emily-Lynn Warren) against permitting a practice associated with a few Islamic immigrant communities. Hall and Warren, "The First Federal Criminal Case on Female Genital Mutilation Will Test the Limits of Religious Liberty," *Learn Liberty*, August 17, 2017, https://www.learnliberty.org/blog/the-first-federal-criminal -case-on-female-genital-mutilation-will-test-the-limits-of-religious-liberty/.
72. Dreisbach and Hall, *Sacred Rights of Conscience*, 388, 394.
73. Dreisbach and Hall, *Sacred Rights of Conscience*, 464.

Conclusion

1. I recognize that my account is not exhaustive. In a sequel to this book, I will respond to critics who claim, among other things, that America did not have a Christian founding because (1) the founders owned slaves and did not abolish slavery, (2) the founders oppressed Native Americans, (3) the War of Independence was unbiblical and unjust, and (4) founding-era Americans were not a "churched" people.
2. *Collected Works of James Wilson*, ed. Kermit L. Hall and Mark David Hall (Indianapolis: Liberty Fund Press, 2007), 1:698.
3. Space constraints prevent me from defining the "common good" here, but it certainly includes things such as protecting innocent human life and preserving religious liberty.
4. Daniel L. Dreisbach and Mark David Hall, eds., *The Sacred Rights of Conscience: Selected Readings on Religious Liberty and Church-State Relations in the American Founding* (Indianapolis: Liberty Fund Press, 2009), 278.

5. Dreisbach and Hall, *Sacred Rights of Conscience*, 278.

6. See, for instance, my essays "A Missed Opportunity: *Masterpiece Cakeshop v. Colorado Civil Rights Commission*," Law and Liberty, June 6, 2018, http://www.libertylawsite.org/2018/06/06/masterpiece-cakeshop-v-colorado-civil-rights-commission/; and "Why Tolerate Religion?" *Citizens and Statesmen: An Annual Review of Political Theory and Public Life* 12 (Fall 2019).

7. I list only those groups with which I have personally worked or interacted. Daniel Bennett provides an excellent overview and analysis of these and related organizations in *Defending Faith: The Politics of the Christian Conservative Legal Movement* (Lawrence: University Press of Kansas, 2017).

ABOUT THE AUTHOR

Mark David Hall is Herbert Hoover Distinguished Professor of Politics and Faculty Fellow in the William Penn Honors Program at George Fox University. He is also associated faculty at the Center for the Study of Law and Religion at Emory University and a senior fellow at Baylor University's Institute for Studies of Religion.

Professor Hall has written, edited, or coedited a dozen books, including *Great Christian Jurists in American History* (New York: Cambridge University Press, 2019); *America and the Just War Tradition: A History of U.S. Conflicts* (Notre Dame: University of Notre Dame Press, 2019); *Faith and the Founders of the American Republic* (New York: Oxford University Press, 2014); *Roger Sherman and the Creation of the American Republic* (New York: Oxford University Press, 2013); *America's Forgotten Founders* (Wilmington: ISI, 2011); *The Forgotten*

Founders on Religion and Public Life (Notre Dame: University of Notre Dame Press, 2009); *The Sacred Rights of Conscience: Selected Readings on Religious Liberty and Church-State Relations in the American Founding* (Indianapolis: Liberty Fund Press, 2009); *The Founders on God and Government* (Lanham: Rowman & Littlefield, 2004); and *The Political and Legal Philosophy of James Wilson, 1742–1798* (Columbia: University of Missouri Press, 1997).